THE BUSINESS CASE FOR STORAGE NETWORKS

Bill Williams

Cisco Press

800 East 96th Street
Indianapolis, Indiana 46240 USA

The Business Case for Storage Networks

Bill Williams
Copyright© 2005 Cisco Systems, Inc.
Published by:
Cisco Press
800 East 96th Street
Indianapolis, IN 46240 USA

Printed in the United States of America 1 2 3 4 5 6 7 8 9 0
First Printing October 2004
Library of Congress Cataloging-in-Publication Number: 2003114112
ISBN: 1-58720-118-6

Warning and Disclaimer

This book is designed to provide information about measuring the total cost of ownership (TCO) for storage networking technologies. Every effort has been made to make this book as complete and as accurate as possible, but no warranty or fitness is implied.

The information is provided on an "as is" basis. The authors, Cisco Press, and Cisco Systems, Inc. shall have neither liability nor responsibility to any person or entity with respect to any loss or damages arising from the information contained in this book or from the use of the discs or programs that may accompany it.

The opinions expressed in this book belong to the author and are not necessarily those of Cisco Systems, Inc.

Corporate and Government Sales

Cisco Press offers excellent discounts on this book when ordered in quantity for bulk purchases or special sales.

For more information, please contact: U.S. Corporate and Government Sales 1-800-382-3419 corpsales@pearsontechgroup.com

For sales outside the U.S., please contact: **International Sales** international@pearsoned.com

Trademark Acknowledgments

All terms mentioned in this book that are known to be trademarks or service marks have been appropriately capitalized. Cisco Press or Cisco Systems, Inc. cannot attest to the accuracy of this information. Use of a term in this book should not be regarded as affecting the validity of any trademark or service mark.

Feedback Information

At Cisco Press, our goal is to create in-depth technical books of the highest quality and value. Each book is crafted with care and precision, undergoing rigorous development that involves the unique expertise of members from the professional technical community.

Readers' feedback is a natural continuation of this process. If you have any comments regarding how we can improve the quality of this book, or otherwise alter it to better suit your needs, you can contact us through email at feedback@ciscopress.com. Please make sure to include the book title and ISBN in your message. We greatly appreciate your assistance.

Publisher   John Wait

Editor-in-Chief   John Kane

Executive Editor   Jim Schachterle

Cisco Representative   Anthony Wolfenden

Cisco Press Program Manager   Nannette M. Noble

Production Manager   Patrick Kanouse

Development Editor   Andrew Cupp

Project and Copy Editor   Ginny Munroe

Technical Editors   Hagen Finley, Philip Lowden, and John Nelsen

Editorial Assistant   Tammi Barnett

Book and Cover Designer   Louisa Adair

Composition   Mark Shirar

Indexer   Julie Bess

CISCO SYSTEMS

Corporate Headquarters
Cisco Systems, Inc.
170 West Tasman Drive
San Jose, CA 95134-1706
USA
www.cisco.com
Tel: 408 526-4000
    800 553-NETS (6387)
Fax: 408 526-4100

European Headquarters
Cisco Systems International BV
Haarlerbergpark
Haarlerbergweg 13-19
1101 CH Amsterdam
The Netherlands
www-europe.cisco.com
Tel: 31 0 20 357 1000
Fax: 31 0 20 357 1100

Americas Headquarters
Cisco Systems, Inc.
170 West Tasman Drive
San Jose, CA 95134-1706
USA
www.cisco.com
Tel: 408 526-7660
Fax: 408 527-0883

Asia Pacific Headquarters
Cisco Systems, Inc.
Capital Tower
168 Robinson Road
#22-01 to #29-01
Singapore 068912
www.cisco.com
Tel: +65 6317 7777
Fax: +65 6317 7799

Cisco Systems has more than 200 offices in the following countries and regions. Addresses, phone numbers, and fax numbers are listed on the
Cisco.com Web site at www.cisco.com/go/offices.

Argentina • Australia • Austria • Belgium • Brazil • Bulgaria • Canada • Chile • China PRC • Colombia • Costa Rica • Croatia • Czech Republic
Denmark • Dubai, UAE • Finland • France • Germany • Greece • Hong Kong SAR • Hungary • India • Indonesia • Ireland • Israel • Italy
Japan • Korea • Luxembourg • Malaysia • Mexico • The Netherlands • New Zealand • Norway • Peru • Philippines • Poland • Portugal
Puerto Rico • Romania • Russia • Saudi Arabia • Scotland • Singapore • Slovakia • Slovenia • South Africa • Spain • Sweden
Switzerland • Taiwan • Thailand • Turkey • Ukraine • United Kingdom • United States • Venezuela • Vietnam • Zimbabwe

About the Author

Bill Williams is the manager of the Cisco Storage Operations Team, where he focuses on storage TCO, metrics, and operational efficiencies. Bill joined Cisco Systems, Inc. in 1998 as an ERP systems administrator. In January, 2002, Bill moved to the Virtual Storage Team at Cisco, where he was integral in creating a dedicated Enterprise Storage Systems Team within Cisco IT. In May 2003, the Enterprise Storage Systems Team won the Cisco CIO Award.

In October, 2002, Bill began studying the TCO for storage at Cisco, and the following year he began a consolidation project to lower storage TCO at Cisco. As the program manager for the Network Storage Virtual Team from 2003 to 2004, Bill guided the implementation of SAN storage and infrastructure in Cisco datacenters around the globe. Bill holds an MBA from the University of North Carolina at Chapel Hill. Bill also holds a master's degree from Harvard Divinity School. Bill lives in Chapel Hill, North Carolina with his wife Lia and their daughter Isabel.

About the Technical Reviewers

Philip Lowden currently holds the position of customer support engineer for storage area networking at Cisco Systems, Inc. Prior to this role, he worked for four years at Cisco and six years at Electronic Data Systems where he was a senior UNIX systems administrator who performed production systems architecture and support duties on a variety of host and storage platforms. He was also an officer in the U.S. Air Force for six years. Philip holds a master's degree in science in computer engineering from North Carolina State University, a bachelor of science degree in computer science from the University of Nebraska, and a bachelor of art degree in English from Saint Meinrad College. He is a SNIA-certified, FC-SAN Specialist. He is married and has two children.

John Nelsen is a member of the Cisco Infrastructure Architecture team and a project manager in the Cisco Systems IT Enterprise Storage Solutions Group. Prior to joining Cisco Systems, John worked for ten years in the pharmaceutical industry, and he has 20 years of experience in various IT architecture and operational roles. When John joined Cisco in 2000, his primary responsibilities included defining and selling a strategy to reduce storage TCO that was founded on the concept of a consolidated storage utility. Since gaining acceptance for the strategy in 2001, John has focused on defining the hardware and software technologies along with the business processes and projects required to build and implement a storage architecture capable of supporting the storage utility. John received his bachelor of science degree from Allegheny College in 1984 and a master's degree in science from North Carolina State University in 1988.

Dedications

I dedicate this book to Lia, Isabel, the animals, and the wonderful life we have together. Thank you for all that you do and all that you are.

Acknowledgments

This book could not have happened without the assistance of every storage administrator, project manager, and executive who shared their story with me. Now more than ever, time is a premium commodity, of which none of us have enough. The fact that so many of you were willing to share your time with me highlights not only the passion that you have for your work, but also the desire in your hearts to help others like yourselves. Even if you were not allowed to speak on the record, you know who you are and your input is recorded here.

Without a doubt, the Cisco Enterprise Storage Services team and its leadership (certainly my manager Scott Zimmer) deserve credit for allowing me to take this project on in addition to all my other responsibilities. Storage strategies and visions mean little without hard work to back them up. Along these same lines, I have to thank John Nelsen, Phil Lowden, and Hagen Finley for reviewing the work at its many stages. Although they might disagree, I believe that reviewing this book (and providing insightful, useful comments) was more difficult a task than writing it. To John I owe a special debt of gratitude for crafting the Cisco Storage Story and for shaping many of the guiding principles behind the storage vision.

It is absolutely critical that I pass along my appreciation for the hard work and cooperation of the staff at IDC. In particular, I want to thank John McArthur and Natalya Yezhkova, who not only assisted me in my research, but also provided a close reading of the first draft and suggestions on how to best use the data provided by IDC.

I also want to thank John Noh, the public relations manager for the Storage Technology Group at Cisco Systems, Inc., for his last minute assistance in helping me review the Cisco case study and for providing me with additional opportunities for publication.

Alison Conigliaro-Hubbard of Cisco and Tom Gelbach of EMC were a tremendous help in lining up contacts for case studies. During the process of writing this book, I talked to numerous storage managers, project managers, and IT directors, but due to the sensitive nature of the material discussed here, many of the individuals I spoke to declined to share data in print. This does not mean that their input is not reflected here. To these individuals, I owe a great deal of thanks. For participating in this project anonymously with very little to show for your time and effort, I thank you.

I also appreciate the assistance of the other researchers whose work is reprinted or referenced here. It is a pleasure to not have to undertake an effort such as this in a vacuum.

I owe a debt of gratitude to Thomas Herbig at McKinsey and Company and Alberto Torres, formerly of McKinsey and Company and now with Nokia, as well as Tim Cannon at Harvard Business School Publishing, for their assistance in fine-tuning the work presented here.

In addition, I would like to offer sincere thanks to the following individuals: Susan Davis, vice president of product marketing and management at Egenera; Nancy Herzog, director of marketing communications at Egenera; Ray Villeneuve, president and CEO of MonoSphere; Mark Davis, vice president of marketing and general manager of customer service and support at MonoSphere; Mike Koclanes, CTO of CreekPath; Scott Hansbury, senior vice president of marketing at CreekPath; Jennifer Roane, senior manager of public relations at CreekPath; Dr. Raphael Yahalom, chief scientist and co-founder of Onaro; and Tom Riddle, vice president of business development at Onaro.

In addition, I want to thank Fred Moore of Horison Inc., Christian Terwiesch of the Wharton School, and authors Jon William Toigo and Nicholas Carr for their knowledge, guidance, and support.

Many thanks to the Cisco Press production team, especially Andrew Cupp, Ginny Munroe, and my editor Jim Schachterle. I have always believed Cisco Press products to be of the highest quality. Having participated in the process for the last 12 months, I can personally attest to the quality of the teams dedicated to the production of Cisco Press materials.

Finally, I want to thank Broad Street Coffee Roasters in Durham, North Carolina and Open Eye Café in the People's Republic of Carrboro. Many a great work can be contributed to great caffeine.

Contents at a Glance

Contents

Foreword

As the 21st century began, the dot-coms dominated almost every initiative in the IT industry, Y2K drove countless irrational actions, businesses were introduced to and sampled the new concept of storage networking, and innovation seemed to be everywhere. Just a few years later, we witnessed the dot-coms' collapse, endured a prolonged recession that was particularly evident in the technology sector, and painfully witnessed the weaknesses in most aspects of security that raised interest in data protection and disaster recovery technologies to unprecedented levels.

The growth of the data storage industry was marked by a steadily increasing trend line that was evident in just about every statistic that could be measured from the early 1970s until late in the year 2000. Often called the Infinite Disruption, the worldwide events of 2001 brought significant changes to the storage industry landscape. Growth rates slowed, worldwide storage revenue declined, thousands of IT jobs were eliminated and many moved offshore, industry consolidation accelerated, and the global economy entered a well-chronicled and lasting slump.

The rate of change for the IT industry, therefore, has slowed from the pre-2001 period. Venture capital and new business ideas are slowly entering the system, further hindering innovation. In 2000, 87 new storage companies were launched with a first round of funding. Today, only business plans that solve real problems are funded. As a result, just two new storage companies were funded in 2003. In 2001, the number of storage firms reporting net losses hit 69 percent. Vendor roadmaps have been pushed out as storage vendors derive lower profitability and, therefore, have less money to invest in the future. The trend for profitability shifted and headed in the right direction as 46 percent reported losses in 2003. A record for the past three years, 79 percent of the companies reporting financials experienced revenue growth in 2003 over 2002. This offers more encouragement. The positive direction is now expected to continue, although unexpected world events continue to temper optimism and make irrational exuberance a thing of the past.

By the end of 2004, a new game with new rules was unfolding. These rules describe a better value system for the storage networking industry; for the first time, the overall value proposition is more important than raw price. Most businesses today still look at the hardware purchase price as the primary purchase criteria. This is increasingly unfortunate and reflects the old and out-of-date viewpoint that hardware is where the value of the IT infrastructure exists. This is like measuring the value of the television industry by the number of sets sold (the old rules) rather than the value of the content transmitted by television (the new rules). With hardware prices falling at 30 to 40 percent annually per unit of storage, the value of the storage industry shifts from atoms to bits.

As a result, the lowest price might not be the best solution for a business and might cost considerably more in the long run. Choosing a solution that provides the optimal overall value, the best return on investment (ROI), Economic Value Added (EVA), or the lowest total cost of ownership (TCO) is replacing the sticker price mentality of the past. The impact of this transformation will have lasting effects, altering much of the traditional thinking and defining a need to more clearly navigate through the next era that awaits the storage industry.

It is doubtful that any visionary could have predicted these events and developed the appropriate responses to deal with the issues in advance. In this book, Bill Williams offers you a valuable and comprehensive set of guidelines and case studies to effectively understand how to lower the TCO for storage while making the business case for storage networks. This excellent work addresses some of the biggest challenges that both users and vendors need to consider when implementing a storage strategy. I highly recommend this book to anyone in search of a better way to implement and manage storage networking infrastructure.

Fred Moore
President, Horison, Inc.
August 2, 2004

Introduction

Events in recent history—most notably the collapse of Enron and MCI/ WorldCom and the September 11th tragedy have precipitated an increased focus on both IT governance and business continuance. Compliance with government regulations, now a priority for most businesses, will dramatically alter the way businesses manage data. This, in turn, will drive further adoption of storage networks and storage networking technologies.

Storage networking technologies, both hardware and software, will have a major impact on the way businesses use IT, on a par with the advent of the local-area network. Early adopters of storage networking technologies have already seen decreases in capital expenditures and increases in operational efficiency as a result of deploying storage networks. Many IT initiatives related to consolidation and business continuance and business continuance are highly dependant on storage networks as a technology enabler. Now more than ever, measuring the financial impact of storage networking is critical to business success.

Demonstrating the value of the storage network rests primarily on the ability to quantify the advantages of implementation and deployment. All too often this analysis is not performed before, during, or even after the solution has been rolled out. It has been my experience that the two most common reasons storage decision makers ignore the financial analysis related to storage network deployments are the lack of time and the lack of experience in formulating the problem.

Goals and Methods

The primary goal of this book is to provide in one resource a general guideline to both storage networking technologies and the financial metrics used for measuring the impact of storage networks on a company's bottom line.

As end users struggle to understand how businesses are impacted by the myriad of new government regulations, they are simultaneously bombarded with discussions of new products and concepts designed to help them better manage storage. This book is intended to help transfer the knowledge I have gained from my own experiences and from my many conversations with business leaders to, in turn, lessen the end user's burden.

Who Should Read This Book?

The Business Case for Storage Networks is written for project managers and technical architects who desire a broader knowledge of financial methods and storage networking technologies. This book is also written for executives and business leaders who seek ways to reduce costs, improve efficiencies, and strengthen business continuance capabilities.

I have found in my conversations with IT leaders, as I mentioned earlier, that the main reason TCO analysis is not done more frequently is because of the shortage of time and the lack of knowledgeable resources to assist in the process. Although this book is not the final word on TCO, the basic data and tools included here should help kick-start TCO analysis and provide a handy reference for frequently used formulas.

End-user case studies included in this book provide crucial, firsthand data from the front lines. Early adopters and mainstream adopters alike can benefit from the stories of businesses that have advanced their corporate IT strategies through the use of storage networks.

How This Book Is Organized

This book is organized into two parts. Part I, "The Storage Networking Value Proposition," is designed to give both a general overview of the storage and storage networking markets, provide a summary of available products and technologies, and supply a detailed discusson of TCO analysis. Related tools and metrics for measuring the financial benefits of strategies designed to lower the storage TCO are also covered in depth in Part I.

NOTE	Please note that for the sake of simplicity throughout the book, I use round numbers or the colloquial totals for numbers of MB, TB, and PB (for example 1000 MB for 1 GB instead of 1024 MB).

Part II, "Case Studies," contains research data compiled from interviews with individuals whose professional lives are consumed with managing storage investments and resources for their companies. During the process of selecting case studies, I sought representation from firms from different sectors, and I believe that the sum total of the data I present here creates a balanced, realistic view of the typical storage consumer. Included in this section are case studies from each of the following verticals: healthcare, retail, manufacturing, financial services, and communications.

NOTE   The case studies were without a doubt the most difficult and taxing portions of the book to write. I interviewed many individuals during the process of writing *The Business Case for Storage Networks*. The majority of the individuals (or their employers) declined publication, in part, due to the sensitivity of the data and how it relates to company performance and the bottom line. This fact alone should attest to the competitive advantage of the storage networking value proposition.

As an indirect result of Cisco Systems entering the Fibre Channel storage market, many of the participating companies who graciously agreed to publish their data are Cisco customers. This should in no way diminish the impact of their experiences or the importance of the information they share.

Although some of the case studies are presented anonymously, in many instances, concrete financial data has been omitted either at the request of the parties involved or because the deployments of storage networks in question are in their infancy, and quantifiable results were forthcoming at the time of publication.

Although financial analysis is a critical component of any case study, the reader is encouraged to also find value in the presentation of data that highlights other key concepts of Part 1 of this book, such as the fact that each company is in a different stage of deploying storage networks, and each company places a different value on the various benefits of networked storage. In addition, it is interesting to note the different methods used for calculating TCO, as well as the fact that some companies are just beginning to consider the benefits of TCO analysis.

The chapters in Part I cover the following topics in detail:

- Chapter 1, "Industry Landscape: Storage Costs and Consumption"— This chapter gives an overview of the rise and fall of technology spending between 1998 and 2003, and it offers some forward-looking analysis on potential storage spending related to current events and developments in U.S. legislation.

- Chapter 2, "The Business Impact of Storage Networking Technology"— This chapter provides a basic overview of the two most important features of networked storage (increased utilization and increased availability) and some of the ways businesses can benefit from implementing a storage network. This chapter covers backup and recovery, replication, and SAN extensions. This chapter also introduces the concept of TCO.

- Chapter 3, "Building a Value Case Using Financial Metrics"—This chapter provides the basic tools for creating a value case: financial metrics. The most commonly used metrics are covered in this chapter: Payback, return-on-investment (ROI), Net Present Value (NPV), and Economic Value Added (EVA). Sample value cases are provided for four storage networking strategies: direct-attached storage to storage-area network (DAS-to-SAN) migration, storage consolidation, direct-attached storage to network-attached storage (DAS-to-NAS) migration, and Internet Small Computer Systems Interface (iSCSI) implementation.

- Chapter 4, "How It Should Be Done: Implementation Strategies and Best Practices"—This chapter begins with a storage technology primer that covers capacity planning and storage networking topologies. This chapter also includes best practices for vendor selection, maintenance, support, and service level management. The chapter concludes with a discussion of job functions and roles.

- Chapter 5, "Maximizing Storage Investments"—This chapter primarily discusses the ongoing maintenance and management of a storage network including the tactical and strategic steps required after implementation. Storage management software and broader consolidation strategies that can assist in achieving and maintaining a low TCO are also covered in this chapter.

Part II contains end-user case studies:

- Chapter 6, "The Cancer Therapy and Research Center"

- Chapter 7, "Internet Service Provider"

- Chapter 8, "Cisco Systems, Inc."

- Chapter 9, "Retail Grocer"

- Chapter 10, "Financial Services"

This book includes three apppendixes that summarize helpful storage networking resources you can find on the Cisco Press website at http://www.ciscopress.com/1587201186:

- Appendix A, "Decision Maker Implementation Checklist"

- Appendix B, "The Business Case for Storage Networks: Storage Strategies for Lowering TCO"

- Appendix C, "TCO Calculator"

CHAPTER 1

INDUSTRY LANDSCAPE: STORAGE COSTS AND CONSUMPTION

Just as the effects of the recent economic downturn have been universally felt across all sectors and industries, likewise do the principle concepts discussed in this chapter—the commoditization of hardware and storage utilization efficiencies—apply to all IT environments, regardless of the size or the nature of the business application. This chapter sets the stage for understanding the storage network as a value-add to the firm insofar as it is capable of alleviating the management and financial burdens associated with direct-attached storage (DAS).

Networked storage offers significant business advantages over DAS, and the impact of these benefits can be quantified and measured. To understand the nature of the business benefits of networked storage, a brief, general discussion of overall IT spending and the specifics of storage spending is required and provides a basis for the remainder of the analysis performed in later chapters.

This chapter covers the following topics:

- Storage management

- Implementing a storage vision

- The commoditization of hardware

- The impact of industry trends and legislation on storage consumption

- Storage utilization, storage yield, and the Cost of Poor Quality (COPQ)

Storage Management Matters

In May, 2003, author Nicholas Carr garnered much attention with a *Harvard Business Review* article on the strategic worth of information technology. The article's provocative title, "IT Doesn't Matter," bespoke Carr's argument that the commoditization of information technology solutions has essentially depleted the strategic advantage of information technology as a whole. In "IT Doesn't Matter," Carr states succinctly, "What makes a resource truly strategic—what gives it the capacity to be the basis for a sustained competitive advantage—is not ubiquity, but scarcity."[1] Carr points to innovations, such as electricity and rail transportation, which offered competitive advantages to early adopters, but whose value diminished over time as the use of these technologies became common place.

In 2004, Carr expanded his position in his book, *Does IT Matter? Information Technology and the Corrosion of Competitive Advantage*, in which he urges readers to decrease IT spending, to avoid being an early adopter whenever possible, and to focus on "vulnerabilities" instead of "opportunities" where critical services are at risk.[2]

Carr could not be more accurate. It is also important to understand, however, that investment in storage networks allows firms to decrease storage spending and focus on service vulnerabilities. In addition, Fibre Channel SANs are well past the early adopt phase. Investment in storage networking technologies (not just Fibre Channel, but IP-based storage solutions as well) can help companies become more efficient and therefore more competitive.

NOTE Everett Rogers originally outlined the concept of the early adopter in his work *The Diffusion of Innovations*. Detailed discussion of Rogers' work and how it applies to product adoption life cycles follows in Chapter 4, "How It Should Be Done: Implementation Strategies and Best Practices."

Understanding competitive forces is a fundamental premise of business leadership. Harvard Business School professor and author Michael Porter is a renowned expert on strategy and competition. He has written extensively on the nature of competition between rival firms and nations. Porter's groundbreaking essay, "How Competitive Forces Shape Strategy," was first published in 1979; twenty-five years later, Porter's "Five Forces," as they have come to be known, still aptly describe the interplay between rival firms' strategic endeavors.

As Porter outlined, the five main forces shaping competition between firms in similar industries are the following:

- Buyer bargaining power
- Supplier bargaining power
- The threat of substitute products
- Rivalry
- Barriers to entry

In his essay, Porter lists "economies of scale" and "cost disadvantages independent of size" as two of the major sources of "barriers to entry."[3] Although "learning curves," "experience curves," and "economies of scale" are concepts typically applied to manufacturing environments, these concepts also have distinct applications in IT, relative to the management of IT assets, and storage assets in particular.

Without a doubt, one of the most significant vulnerabilities facing companies today is the state of enterprise storage, now in overwhelming disarray following the deployment at breakneck speed of over two million DAS external disk units worldwide between the years of 1999 and 2003. The total number of DAS versus networked storage units sold between 1999 and 2003 is shown in Table 1-1.

Table 1-1   *Worldwide External Non-OEM Factory Revenue ($M) and Shipments, 1999-2003 (Source: IDC, 2004)[4]*

Worldwide External Non-OEM Factory Revenue ($M) and Shipments, 1999-2003					
	2003	2002	2001	2000	1999
	$M	$M	$M	$M	$M
DAS	$5504	$5932	$9357	$14,452	$13,773
DAS Units	270,379	298,264	425,255	509,667	503,608
Networked*	$8087	$7165	$7838	$7299	$4368
Networked Units	128,599	141,148	140,902	138,455	74,215

*Denotes SAN and NAS storage.

Jon William Toigo outlined the storage management problem facing IT managers in his book, *The Holy Grail of Storage Management*, published in 2000. Toigo stated clearly and early on that corporate IT departments would face serious challenges in the coming years with managing data storage. The need for online or near-online data and the lack of a rational strategy for dealing with storage growth indicated that in a short amount of time, companies would have their hands full of storage problems.[5] Few in corporate IT today are in a position to disagree with Toigo.

Storage networks allow firms to drive down operational costs and increase economies of scale to remain competitive. At the same time, storage networks allow firms to address critical business vulnerabilities. Although storage networks alone do not magically solve all storage-related problems, a networked storage infrastructure does help increase operational and utilization efficiencies, which ultimately lowers the overall storage total cost of ownership (TCO).

NOTE   Storage networks do not intrinsically solve the problems related to data and information management, but in later chapters I demonstrate how economies of scale with regard to storage management (and the cost advantages of increased storage utilization) have a significant impact on the firm's bottom line.

NOTE   The ubiquity of information technology resources in corporate datacenters underscores the drop in prices for IT products and the diminished magnitude of the capital outlays required to build an enterprise-level IT infrastructure. This ubiquity is the tangible evidence—the hangover, if you will—from the party that heralded the advent of the New Economy.

Implementing a Storage Vision

Now, more than ever, companies are adopting storage networks as fundamental building blocks of a storage vision that addresses the capacity, utilization, and management issues related to data storage. This broader strategy or vision is designed to:

- Reduce the overhead associated with providing storage solutions

- Maximize critical business continuance capabilities

- Increase the performance and flexibility of the overall data storage infrastructure

A storage vision begins with the migration to storage networks, and proceeds with the decommissioning of DAS. A storage vision also requires the classification of environments into tiers and the creation of a service-level framework to measure the efficacy and performance of storage-related deliverables. A storage vision culminates in the ability to provide storage services in a utility-like fashion. The net effect of a storage vision is an overall lower TCO for storage.

The need for low-cost, highly-available storage solutions, coupled with the high demand for long-distance replication functionality (spurred by legislation and security concerns), has helped to increase sales of Fibre Channel (FC) storage networking and optical transport products. This increase in product sales occurred even as disk revenues fell dramatically in 2001 and 2002. The management burden of DAS and the difficulties of managing heterogeneous storage on an FC storage network have led to an increased interest in IP storage networks. It is the belief of some vendors that a strong Fibre Channel infrastructure facilitates the adoption of Internet Small Computer Systems Interface (iSCSI), Fibre Channel over IP (FCIP), and IP over Fibre Channel (IPFC).

The soft economic climate of the last three years has fostered the realization that not every application requires five-star accommodations. Application environments are now consolidated to conserve resources. Likewise, business processes are now modified to provide service-level management (SLM) frameworks that match an application's needs to the most appropriate and cost-efficient storage solution. Service-level management is an increasingly important concept in storage management, and, as shown in the case studies in Part II, "Case Studies," SLM forms the framework around which solid storage visions are currently built.

Five years ago, the typical IT department was asked to provide the most expensive server and disk solutions for every conceivable array of applications. At that time, it was customary for IT departments to provide storage capacity based on poorly scoped application requirements. Then, it was acceptable for IT to serve strictly as a cost center. Those days are over. Now, the focus is on cutting costs at a time when legislation and competition actually create new requirements and drive increased costs. In addition, data storage is growing at such a rate that cutting costs without a storage management strategy is almost impossible.

To understand the importance of a storage vision, it is necessary to look at broader trends in the market. An analysis of the overall storage and IT spending rates for the last several years is illustrative of the current storage management headache facing today's IT decision maker.

Irrational Exuberance

It is no secret that corporate spending on information technology hardware, software, and services has slowed dramatically in recent time. If the drop-off in IT spending was dramatic, the run-up previous to the decline was equally spectacular.

No doubt, times have changed and just as electronic commerce and web technologies have matured, business leaders now understand the importance of value case analysis, and are returning to Net Present Value (NPV) and return on investment (ROI) as methods for validating new IT investments.

The "irrational exuberance" in the securities markets of the late 1990s, noticed as early as 1996 by Federal Reserve Chairman Alan Greenspan, presented significant hurdles to planners, analysts, and those in charge of charting the path of the U.S. economy.[6] This exuberance was fueled in part by Y2K and in part by the multi-million dollar IT budgets burning a hole in the pockets of both Fortune 500 companies and start-ups alike. These firms together shared the collective aim of gaining both a long-term boost in productivity and a competitive edge in the marketplace. The churn-and-burn mentality of the start-ups and dot-coms led to massive capital purchases, inflating the revenues of almost every high-tech company in the value chain.

Table 1-2 clearly shows that one of the primary areas to benefit from exuberant IT spending during this time frame was external disk storage, as highlighted by the increases in vendor revenues between 1999 and 2000.

Table 1-2   *Worldwide External Disk Storage Systems Non-OEM Factory Revenue ($M) and Units, 1999-2003 (Source: IDC, 2004)[7]*

Worldwide External Disk Storage Systems Non-OEM Factory Revenue ($M) and Units, 1999-2003					
	2003	2002	2001	2000	1999
	$M	$M	$M	$M	$M
External Disk Storage Systems	$13,591	$13,097	$17,195	$21,751	$18,141
Units	398,978	439,412	566,157	648,121	577,823

These figures are sufficiently eye-opening in that they highlight the marked increase and then sudden decline in overall revenues. Aside from highlighting a precipitous drop in margins, the unit numbers in Table 1-2, coupled with the percentage of DAS sold worldwide during the same timeframe (as shown in Table 1-1), indicate that there is a mountain of DAS currently deployed.

NOTE   As shown in Table 1-1, 87 percent of supplier revenues in 1999 and 78 percent of supplier revenues in 2000 were from sales of DAS solutions.

As is well documented by now, the "damn-the-ROI" mentality prevailed in IT spending until a series of events accelerated the well-known recent economic downturn.

Macro Sources of Economic Downturn

With capital spending trending downwards, many firms began to report disappointing revenues in late 2000 and early 2001. Of those reporting declines, arguably one of the most significant was Cisco Systems.

On February 7, 2001, Cisco Systems missed its quarterly earnings estimates for the first time in almost three years. Cisco Systems, technology bellwether, and long-time advocate of the virtual close-a process that allowed earnings snapshots to be retrieved at any time to provide guidance to its leadership-came up short of analysts' per share expectations for the second quarter of fiscal year 2001. The subsequent write-down of $2.2 billion worth of Cisco inventory sent shockwaves through its supply chain and had a deleterious effect across the industry.[8] Companies in many sectors questioned their capability to forecast sales and profitability, shareholders suffered, and visibility into U.S. economic recovery became even murkier.

On September 11, 2001, terrorists attacked the World Trade Center and the Pentagon, killing almost 3000 people. The New York Stock Exchange, NASDAQ, and AMEX exchanges were closed for four days. An already shaky U.S. economy found itself against the ropes, and the United States prepared for a multi-front war. Subsequent foreign intervention (in Afghanistan and eventually Iraq) dampened hopes that an economic upswing was imminent, and six cuts in the federal fund rate (one each in the remaining months of 2001 after the September 11 attacks, and one each in 2002 and 2003), shown in Figure 1-1, indicated that the Federal Open Market Committee (the Federal Reserve) saw little sign of economic revival, equally thwarting hopes of a recovery.

Figure 1-1   *Federal Fund Rate Cuts Since January 1, 2000*

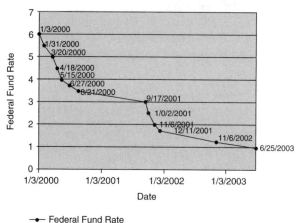

NOTE	On June 30, 2004, the Federal Open Market Committee raised the federal fund rate by one-quarter of one point—its first rate hike in four years.

Data from the Bureau of Economic Analysis highlights the effect of decreased spending for electronic hardware on the U.S. Gross Domestic Product (GDP) during the period in question (shown in Figure 1-2).[9]

Figure 1-2 *Electronic and Electric Equipment Manufacturing Contribution to U.S. GDP 1992-2001*

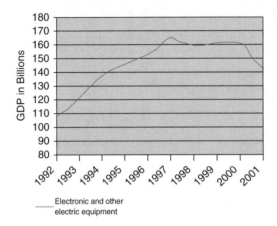

Electronic and other electric equipment

Analysis of the effects of economic growth related to the "New Economy" began in October, 2001, when the McKinsey Global Institute released its study titled "U.S. Productivity Growth 1995-2000." This study indicated that although IT spending increased between 1995 and 2000, IT was just one of several factors (including innovation, cyclical demand, and competition) contributing to U.S. productivity growth during this time frame.[10]

Some point to this "productivity paradox," as it has come to be called, as highlighting the failure of corporate spending on IT products and services to lead to a tangible increase in sustained output of U.S. companies. Although this point is debatable, what is clear is the subsequent decrease in profits for major storage and server vendors, indicating the commoditization of both the disk and the host.

NOTE	Whether or not the economic downturn was officially a recession, there seems to be little doubt at this point. In July, 2003, the National Bureau of Economic Research (NBER) issued a report stating that the last U.S. recession ended in November, 2001. The NBER's Business Cycle Dating Committee, which tracks the timelines of U.S. business cycles, pinned the length of this most recent recession, which began in March, 2001, at eight months, three less than the post-World War II average of 11 months.[11]

Commoditization of Hardware

So, what were the long-term effects of the "New Economy?" This is the subject of heated debate; however, economists J. Bradford DeLong and Lawrence Summers provide us with an insight into one aspect of the "New Economy:" competition. In an address at Kansas City's Federal Reserve Bank Symposium in August, 2001, DeLong and Summers argued that the long-term effects of the technological advances of the "New Economy" would not be the creation of "scale-related cost advantages," but the creation instead of a more level playing field, making competition itself "more effective."[12]

Obviously DeLong and Summers refer primarily to the supply side of the economic equation. Accordingly, they state, "Competitive edges based on past reputations, or brand loyalty, or advertising footprints will fade away. As they do so, profit margins will fall: Competition will become swifter, stronger, more pervasive, and more nearly perfect. Consumers will gain and shareholders will lose."[13]

The commoditization of disk and server hardware is therefore a visible symptom of stronger and more perfect competition, and certainly the consumer in most circumstances benefits from increased purchasing power. The question, however, remains: Do the consumers gain a true advantage? Not if the commoditized assets are poorly utilized, which, when dealing with storage, is more often than not, the unfortunate case.

The Disk as Commodity

As noted, IT spending on the whole declined dramatically between the years 2000 and 2003, and the effect on the disk storage industry has been punishing. IT spending began to suffer in some cases as early as 1999, but the disk storage industry shows itself to be a lagging indicator of decreased corporate spending. The delayed decline of storage revenues were due in part to poor utilization efficiencies, which buffeted disk spending by forcing companies to purchase more storage.

The increased revenues for disk storage systems between the years of 1999 and 2000 (as shown in Table 1-2) were primarily due to three factors:

- Spending on Y2K-related infrastructure

- Continued demand for web and electronic commerce applications

- Increases in the number of complex enterprise resource planning and supply-chain management installations

As a major manufacturer of disk storage systems and a provider of disk-related software and services, the annual revenues for the Hopkinton, Massachusetts-based firm, EMC Corporation, provide an excellent snapshot of disk spending for the two years on either side of Y2K (shown in Figure 1-3).

Figure 1-3 *EMC Annual Revenues from 1998–2002*[14]

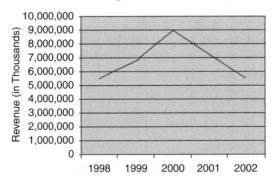

What is more germane to the premise of this discussion, however, is the breakdown of revenue by line of business at EMC Corporation from 2000 to 2003 (see Figure 1-4). These figures show at a glance the growing shift in focus from disk sales to revenue generation through software and services. This shift indicates further commoditization of disk storage.

Figure 1-4   *Percentage of EMC Revenue by Line of Business[15]*

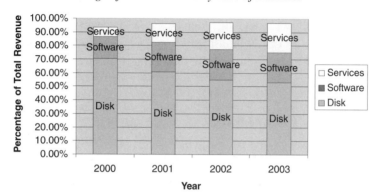

NOTE	Note that the software figures exclude revenues from Legato and Documentum because the acquisition of these two firms occurred midway through the 2003 financial year (in October and December, 2003, respectively).

It is important for the purposes of this discussion not only to note the contraction in revenues and units sold for disk storage systems, as previously shown, but also to note the steady increase in sales of Fibre Channel infrastructure components as outlined in Table 1-3.

Table 1-3   *Worldwide Fibre Channel Switches and HBAs Factory Revenue ($M), 2000–2003 (Source IDC, 2004).[16]*

Worldwide Fibre Channel Switches and HBAs Factory Revenue ($M), 2000-2003				
	2003	2002	2001	2000
WW FC Switches and HBAs	$1673	$1448	$1346	$1181

Three consecutive years of growth in the Fibre Channel switch market point to a shift from DAS to SAN infrastructure and, as intelligence moves onto the storage network, the commoditization of disk storage continues.

The Server as Commodity

Server sales decreased dramatically between 2000 and 2002. The number of server units sold during this same time frame indicates the increased commoditization of the host.

Table 1-4 shows the decrease in worldwide server revenues between 2000 and 2002, echoing the trend evidenced previously in the storage numbers. These figures also show the relative plateau in the number of units shipped during this same period. The 2003 spike in revenues and units sold highlights decreased margins and the move to lower-priced, rack-mountable server platforms, further illustrating the trend toward commoditization.

Table 1-4   *Worldwide Server Factory Revenue ($M) and Units Shipped from 1999–2003 (Sources: IDC 2004 Release)[17]*

Worldwide Server Factory Revenue ($M) and Units Shipped					
	2003	2002	2001	2000	1999
	$M	$M	$M	$M	$M
WW Total	$46,131	$44,649	$50,496	$61,675	$57,708
Units	5,281,231	4,442,690	4,276,119	4,369,840	3,761,141

NOTE   The increased popularity of rack-mountable servers stems from the capability to provide enterprise-class service for a fraction of the cost and the footprint. More rack-mountable server deployments, however, translate into increased datacenter costs in terms of management efficiencies.

Blade servers have the potential to alleviate the pain points associated with implementing significant numbers of rack-mountable servers. Rack-mountable servers tend to overwhelm the datacenter with network, power, cooling, and storage demands, whereas blade servers can utilize shared datacenter resources to cut back on the capacity consumed per deployment.

Additional discussion of blade servers and virtualization of disk and CPU resources follows in Chapter 5, "Maximizing Storage Investments."

It is reasonable to assume that the adoption of the Linux operating system has also contributed to the commoditization of the server.

An application infrastructure based on the Linux operating system has a significantly lower TCO than one based on a proprietary operating system. The increased customer adoption rate of Linux will continue to apply pressure on companies whose revenues are derived from sales of proprietary operating systems and enterprise-class servers.

The Impact of Competition on IT

As previously seen, a number of industry trends and current events have helped to shape IT spending over the last three years. The worldwide storage market (which includes sales of disk, software, and storage-related services) now constitutes more than $40 billion of business and, despite the commoditization of disk storage, showed signs of recovery in 2003. Table 1-5 highlights recent increases in revenues for storage software and services.

Table 1-5 *Worldwide Storage Software and Services Market ($M), 1999–2003 (Source: IDC, 2004)[18]*

Worldwide Storage Software and Services Market ($M), 1999-2003					
	2003	2002	2001	2000	1999
Storage Software	$6621	$5730	$6157	$6113	$4640
Storage Services	$23,360	$21,171	$20,552	$19,501	$17,250

While disk sales notched a nearly four percent increase in 2003 (see Table 1-2), sales of storage software and services were more robust. Sales of storage software in 2003 increased nearly 16 percent over 2002, whereas sales of storage services increased more than 10 percent over the previous year.

As worldwide server revenues indicate, after two consecutive years of double-digit declines, server sales also experienced a slight uptick of 3 percent in 2003 (see Table 1-4).

Recent increases in IT spending are now driven by companies seeking both a competitive edge in the marketplace and compliance with new laws and regulations stemming from current events.

Despite the lack of a clear correlation between IT spending and profitability, increased competition in every sector forces companies to continue to seek ways to use IT to create a competitive advantage. The advantage of IT, as envisioned during the dot-com era, no longer exists. IT is now correctly seen as the framework around which solid business strategies are built.

These strategies are executed primarily through one or more of these four tactics:

- Electronic commerce
- Enterprise resource planning (ERP)
- Supply chain management (SCM)
- Customer relationship management (CRM)

Each of these solutions requires significant investment in storage infrastructure, server resources, and disaster-recovery capabilities.

Electronic commerce has profoundly changed the face of the retail industry. Many traditional brick-and-mortar businesses are now "brick-and-click" businesses that require around-the-clock availability. These environments demand high performance servers and terabytes of storage to house logs for millions of website hits and queries.

In August of 2003, The Economics and Statistics Administration of the U.S. Census Bureau announced an uptick in e-commerce retail spending of 27.8 percent over the previous year. These figures indicate a 214 percent increase in e-commerce retail sales since the fourth quarter of 1999.[19] Similarly, figures for the first quarter of 2004 showed an increase of 28.1 percent over the first quarter of 2003.[20]

Although consumer retail e-commerce is growing, the overwhelming majority of e-commerce transactions are still between businesses. According to data from the U.S. Census Bureau, 93.3 percent of e-commerce sales in 2001 and 93.9 percent in 2000 were business-to-business (B-to-B) transactions. This percentage, however, reflects only 7.3 percent of all traditional B-to-B and business-to-customer (B-to-C) shipments and revenues (or only $1,066 billion out of $14,572 billion) in the United States.[21] These statistics indicate there is still significant room for growth in e-commerce markets.

Similar to e-commerce environments, ERP applications (which often connect to complex e-commerce infrastructures) demand high performance and high availability, as well as replication capabilities. In addition to increased requirements for enterprise class storage, these environments also need massive amounts of storage for the frequent migration and redeployment of application code-trees.

SCM and CRM environments—although extremely different from each other in terms of business functions—have similar high availability requirements and strict performance specifications. As electronic commerce continues to show steady growth, demand planning and call-center capabilities, along with other SCM and CRM functions, become more important. Manufacturing and sales support functions, therefore, now have availability requirements comparable to those of ERP and e-commerce systems.

In addition, the discussion of the business application of IT is incomplete without some mention of email, the foundation of business communication in the 21st century. Although most emails are relatively small in size, the inclusion of attachments in emails greatly increases the burden on backup and storage environments. Regulatory trends and recent legislation dictate the lengthening of email retention policies, which in turn increases the TCO for storage.

Finally, a surge in demand for business process management (BPM) software and ERP software add-ons designed to simplify the process of compliance with complex regulations indicates businesses are coming to terms with compliance with new legislation.

The Impact of Legislation on IT

Several new regulations and acts of legislation will likely increase the corporate data growth rate and will most assuredly change the way companies manage storage resources.

As the following examples indicate, the standard operating procedures of business are changing, and the impact of these changes on financial services and healthcare business systems will be significant, particularly on downstream functions of the storage value chain (offsite data storage, storage-related professional services, and so on).

Regulation Fair Disclosure

When the bull market of the late 1990s was capped off with the NASDAQ crash and the deflation of the Internet bubble, a sobering and humbling string of corporate scandals surfaced just in time to keep the bad news flowing. With the passage of Regulation Fair Disclosure in 2000, the SEC instituted, at least on paper, the first in a long series of efforts designed to limit the ability of the firm and its management to run amok.

In this particular case, "Reg. FD," as it came to be known, outlined a process for limiting publicly traded companies' exposure to the likelihood of insider training. Although Reg. FD forced companies to make the same quality of data available to both analysts and the public simultaneously, authorities did not seek to actively prosecute violators until mid-2001 when cease-and-desist actions were levied against several companies for both intentional and unintentional violations of the regulation. Of course, these actions were obscured a short time later by the activities surrounding the MCI-WorldCom and Enron scandals.

Sarbanes-Oxley

To provide stringent guidelines for corporate governance and in direct response to the debacles at MCI-WorldCom and Enron, the United States Congress passed the Sarbanes-Oxley Act in the summer of 2002. In addition to requiring senior corporate officers to certify financial reports (section 302), blocking personal loans to executive personnel (section 402), and forcing the documentation of internal processes and controls (section 404), the Sarbanes-Oxley Act has potentially far-reaching ramifications to the way companies manage data.

One section of the law—section 409—has the potential to cause significant disruption in current data management policies. In particular, section 409 requires enabling real-time disclosure of pertinent financial data. The impact of this legislation on businesses is such that requirements for storage capacity are likely to increase. Interest in content-addressed storage (CAS) has already increased primarily because of its capability to provide easy access to archived data based on key words and content-specific retention requirements. Compliance with Sarbanes-Oxley will increase sales of networked storage and CAS devices in the near-term.

Health Insurance Portability and Accountability Act of 1996

In addition to Sarbanes-Oxley, the Health Insurance Portability and Accountability Act of 1996 (HIPAA), which serves to make available to every patient in the United States his or her own medical records ("Protected Health Information"), creates a standard interface for the transfer of medical data to ensure privacy and security. HIPAA also establishes measures of accountability in the healthcare industry. Not only does HIPAA complicate backup and retention procedures, however, but it also increases storage consumption rates. As the compliance dates approach, and even the smallest healthcare offices are required to demonstrate some disaster contingency capabilities, storage sales will increase.

NOTE	It is difficult to imagine the amount of data comprising the "Protected Health Information" of every prescription, dental, and medical record of every U.S. citizen. HIPAA requires healthcare providers to keep multiple copies of and lengthen the retention periods for every billing and medical record for every person receiving healthcare services in the United States. That's a lot of data!

Numerous other updated regulations, as well as the aggressive enforcement of laws already on the books, will cause even more headaches for storage consumers while serving to buffer disk manufacturers from a more precipitous drop in revenues.

Title 21

The Title 21 Code of Federal Regulations (21 CFR Part 11), which was issued by the U.S. Food and Drug Administration and announced in August, 2002, promises to streamline the current process for the manufacturing of pharmaceutical products. At the same time, however, Title 21 mandates extension of periods for record-retention. In all likelihood, Title 21 will cause wrinkles in data management programs in most pharmaceutical companies and potentially increase sales of disk devices over time.

Securities and Exchange Commission

Also in August, 2002, the Securities Exchange Commission, together with the Board of Governors of the U.S. Federal Reserve and the Office of the Comptroller of the Currency, issued a request for comments on a draft of a white paper outlining "sound practices" designed to strengthen the infrastructure of the U.S. financial markets.

As a review of lessons learned from the September 11 attacks, the document outlines the lack of controls and processes required to increase business continuance capabilities. The document highlights the need for "rapid recovery and timely resumption" of "critical operations" in the event of catastrophic loss of local or regional disruption, particularly with regard to "core clearing and settlement" organizations whose outages present a "systemic risk" to the stability of the market as a whole.[22]

The "sound practices" outlined in the document specify the need for identification of critical services and the testing of recovery systems in as timely and as cost-effectively a manner as possible. Most significant in the document is the recommendation that companies providing core financial services implement backup strategies so that time-to-recover and distance functions extend well beyond the capabilities provided by current solutions. The draft of the white paper suggests distances of 200–300 miles for "out-of-region" backup facilities and recovery time objectives of typically same-day at a minimum, if not within a few hours.[23]

In April, 2003, the interagency group published the white paper and a summary of comments received. Although it is obvious that there is rigorous debate about what constitutes achievable recovery objectives and realistic distance requirements, based on cost-benefit analyses and the technical capabilities of solutions currently available on the market, one thing is clear: The writing is on the wall. The SEC suggests that organizations that perform "core clearing and settlement functions" continue to work toward having these "sound practices" implemented as soon as the end of 2004, and companies that "play significant roles" (those companies who settle or clear five percent or more of the market) should have similar guidelines implemented within three years of the release of the paper.[24]

In December, 2002, the New York Stock Exchange (NYSE), the National Association of Securities Dealers (NASD), and the SEC, in a joint legal action, levied a total of $8,250,000 in fines against five broker-dealers (Salomon Smith Barney Inc., U.S. Bancorp Piper Jaffray Inc., Goldman, Sachs and Company, Morgan Stanley & Co. Inc, and Deutsche Bank Securities Inc.) for failure to keep communications, in this case electronic mail, in an "accessible place" for the two years stipulated by SEC Rule 17a-4 of the 1934 Securities Exchange Act.[25]

Without a doubt, governmental and corporate IT centers find that living with disaster recovery policies and becoming or remaining compliant with current and updated legislation requires a cohesive storage vision to avoid runaway costs and a management nightmare comprised of expensive and poorly utilized storage.

Current and future legislation is also in a position to further decrease storage utilization, thereby increasing the storage TCO for many consumers. The following section explains the impact of poor utilization.

Utilization and Yield

A fundamental piece of the storage TCO equation is utilization and its direct correlation to what can be referred to as the storage yield. If one assumes that the average company used at best 50 percent of their storage assets between 1999 and 2002 (which is itself a conservative number), then, based on the worldwide revenues shown in Table 1-2, we can estimate that over $35 billion dollars in storage assets went unutilized during that time.

NOTE   In this section, I borrow two terms from different fields—the COPQ (from Total Quality Management and Six-Sigma) and yield (from manufacturing and agriculture)—and I apply those terms to the discussion of storage utilization.

Storage utilization is the most important storage management issue today: Poor utilization wastes millions of dollars a year in unused storage assets.

Understanding utilization is crucial for the introduction of ROI, Net Present Value (NPV), and TCO in Chapter 3, "Building a Value Case Using Financial Metrics." This material is required to build the financial models with which the business case for storage networks can be justified.

A close analysis of storage yield and the COPQ demonstrates how increased utilization helps lower the overall storage TCO.

The Cost of Poor Quality and the Storage Problem

The Cost of Poor Quality, in terms of quality and yield management, typically refers to the costs associated with poor or undesirable performance of a product over the course of its economic usefulness.[26]

A high COPQ implies higher manufacturing, operations, and labor costs, and consequently, lower revenues. Couching the value of an IT solution in terms of quality management, the COPQ can be said to be the dollar value of how a product, service, or solution performs relative to its expectations. In terms of financial analysis, this figure equates to a negative ROI.

Just as the buildup of IT capacity and subsequent downturn was the outcome of macroeconomic events, the move to storage networks is part of many corporations' efforts to raise their storage yield over time and lower the COPQ (and the TCO) for their storage infrastructure.

Storage Yield

In manufacturing operations, the term yield refers to the ratio of good output to gross output.[27] In storage operations as in manufacturing, the yield is never be 100 percent as there is always be some waste. The goal of a storage vision is to increase not only storage yields, which can be measured in dollars or percent of labor, but also to increase operational yields (or "good output") as much as possible. Ultimately, a storage vision built on a storage utility model helps increase a company's storage yield, the amount of storage capacity allocated and then used efficiently to create and sustain business value.

A tiered storage infrastructure is required to fully increase storage yield and gain true economies of scale. In Table 1-5, each tier has a different capability model and different direct and indirect costs associated with it. The goal is for the COPQ to be as insignificant as possible (shown here as a percentage of $1,000,000 in revenue), and ideally for the accompanying tiers to be appropriately matched to the level of business impact or business revenue of the associated applications. A typical tiered storage infrastructure might look something like this:

- Tier One—Mirrored, redundant storage devices with local and remote replication

- Tier Two—RAID-protected, non-redundant storage devices with multiple paths

- Tier Three—Non-protected, non-redundant, near-line storage devices (for example, SATA drives used as a tape replacement)

Table 1-6 *Cost of Poor Quality as a Percentage of $1,000,000 of Revenue for 1000 GB*

Storage Type	Cost per MB	GB	Total Cost	Allocated	Utilized
Tier 1	$0.05	1000	$51,200	80%	75%
Tier 2	$0.03	1000	$30,720	80%	60%
Tier 3	$0.01	1000	$10,240	80%	90%

Storage Type	Allocated Yield	Utilized Yield	Realized Yield	Cost of Poor Quality	COPQ % of Revenue
Tier 1	$40,960	$30,720	60%	$20,480	2.05%
Tier 2	$24,576	$14,746	48%	$15,974	1.60%
Tier 3	$8192	$7373	72%	$2867	0.29%

As seen, a low storage yield has a corresponding high COPQ and indicates an overall higher total cost of storage ownership. A more complete discussion of tiered storage solutions (and Information Lifecycle Management) is presented in Chapter 5.

NOTE The difference between allocated and utilized storage is discussed in the section titled "Utilization."

Obstacles Inherent in DAS

As the predominant storage architecture to date in terms of terabytes deployed, DAS has served the storage needs for millions of environments around the globe. Small Computer Systems Interface (SCSI), DAS is a standard, reliable method of presenting disk to hosts. DAS also presents many challenges to the end user including failover and distance limitations, as well as the increased expense associated with poor utilization.

Failover Limitations

Although some DAS environments are Fibre Channel, large storage environments in open systems datacenters have historically been direct-attached SCSI. SCSI is a mainstream technology that has worked well and has been widely available since the early 1980s. SCSI provided the necessary throughput and was robust enough to get the job done. One disadvantage, however, has always been the inability of the UNIX operating system and most databases to tolerate disruptions in SCSI signals, thus limiting the capability to failover from one path to another without impact to the host. In addition, logical unit number (LUN) assignments are typically loaded into the UNIX kernel when the system is booted up, requiring allocation or de-allocation of storage from the host to be planned during an outage window. If the storage unit in question is shared between different clients with mismatched service-level agreements and different maintenance windows, then negotiating an outage window quickly becomes a hopelessly Sisyphean task.

Distance Limitations

Another significant factor hampering the flexibility of SCSI DAS is that SCSI is limited in its capability to transfer data over significant distances. High Voltage Differential (HVD) SCSI can carry data only up to 25 meters without the aid of SCSI extenders. This limitation presents difficulties for applications requiring long-distance transfer, whether for the purposes of disaster recovery planning, application latency, or just for the more physical logistics of datacenter planning.

Expense

Aside from the technical limitations of DAS, the primary drawback of DAS is, without a doubt, its expense. Ultimately, the storage frames themselves constitute a single point of failure, and to build redundancy into direct-attached systems, it is often necessary to mirror the entire frame, thereby doubling the capital costs of implementation and increasing the management overhead (and datacenter space) required to support the environment.

The expense of DAS also stems from poor utilization rates. A closer look at the two primary types of storage utilization further illustrates the nature of the cost savings inherent in networked storage solutions.

Utilization

When considering the impact of managing storage in general and the financial disadvantages of DAS in particular, the primary variable to monitor is storage utilization. Poor utilization leads to a decreased storage yield and a high COPQ, whereby the storage capital asset purchased to provide a service, fails to perform at an optimal level.

Storage utilization has been a marketing hot-button since Fibre Channel SANs began to gain momentum, and as such, utilization is now laden with many different meanings, all of which are often (and unfortunately) used interchangeably. To prevent further confusion, I prefer to use Jon William Toigo's terminology of efficiencies. Toigo clearly delineates between "allocation efficiency" (broadly referred to as "utilization") and "utilization efficiency," which typically reflects the effects of storage usage policies.[28]

Allocation Efficiency

Due to the physical constraints of the solution, DAS environments are intrinsically susceptible to low "allocation efficiency" rates that cost firms money in terms of unallocated or wasted storage. Let us look at one example of the financial impact of poor allocation efficiency.

Imagine a disk storage system (containing 96 73-GB disk drives) with six four-port SCSI (or Fibre Channel) adapters capable of supporting up to 24 single-path host connections. This system is capable of providing approximately 7008 GB of raw storage, or 3504 GB mirrored. Under most circumstances, hosts have at least two paths to disk, so this particular environment can support a maximum of twelve hosts. In a typical scenario, shown in Figure 1-5, this frame hosts the storage for a small server farm of six clustered hosts (12 nodes).

Figure 1-5   *Sample DAS Configuration*

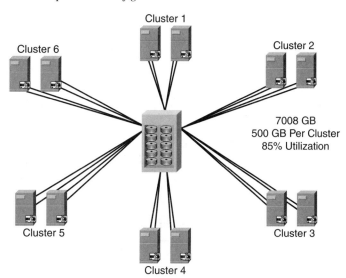

If each cluster hosts six similar applications using 500 GB each (an allocation efficiency rate of 85 percent), almost 500 GB remains unallocated due to the frame's port limitations. With a purchase price of $0.10 per MB, or $100 per GB, there is a loss of $105,120.00 associated with the unutilized disk on that frame.

NOTE   Keep in mind that as this frame is formatted for mirroring, the value of the unallocated storage is the cost of the total non-mirrored storage. In other words, the 500 GB of unallocated storage is still 1 TB raw, which must be valued at its purchase price. Also note that use the $0.10 per MB for quick math. The average purchase price of the disk might be significantly lower.

This loss can be considered the COPQ and reflects the costs of additional storage required to provide the expected capacity. An allocation efficiency rate of 85 percent for a DAS environment, however, is significantly higher than the normal average. In June, 2001, a joint study published by McKinsey & Company and Merrill Lynch's Technology Group, titled "The Storage Report—Customer Perspectives & Industry Evolution," estimated the average utilization rate for DAS environments to be 50 percent.[29]

Fred Moore of Horison Information Strategies has an even more dismal view of allocation efficiency. According to Moore, surveys of clients across various industries indicate allocation efficiencies of 30–40 percent for UNIX and Linux environments and even less for Windows environments, which Moore says frequently see allocation efficiency rates as low as 20 percent.[30]

Using the same environment shown in Figure 1-5 as an example, if the allocation efficiency is only 50 percent, then the loss widens significantly to $350,400, or half the purchase price of the frame. Figure 1-6 shows the costs associated with poor utilization in this environment.

Figure 1-6 *Utilization Rate and Associated Costs—Cash Basis*

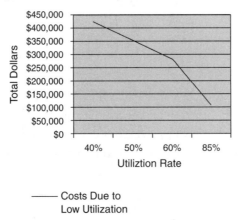

———— Costs Due to
Low Utilization

Most firms depreciate the cost of storage over the course of its useful life (assuming the storage is purchased and not leased), so the actual COPQ might vary according to depreciation schedules.

Given the rapid progress of technological advancement, in most cases, depreciation is carried out over three years. If the straight-line method of depreciation is used over a period of three years, the asset value or purchase price of the frame is divided by three with the assumption that one-third of its usefulness is consumed each year. The impact of the loss, or the COPQ, is then spread across the span of the economic usefulness of the asset. In other words, one third of the COPQ affects the firm's bottom line each year.

Low utilization does not increase or decrease the estimated life of the hardware, nor does this loss change the asset's value in accounting terms. Low utilization does, however, decrease the storage yield of the asset and increases the COPQ, which, in turn, increases the overall TCO. Regardless of the method of depreciation used, poor utilization detracts from the firm's bottom line.

Whether or not the storage units themselves are depreciated, the net effects of poor allocation efficiency are similar: Low allocation efficiency increases the rate of frequency of additional storage purchases. A real life parallel is buying a full tank of gas and being able to use only half of the purchased fuel. As long as you need to drive the car, you will need to purchase more fuel. If more fuel is not consumed, you will be forced to stop at the gas station more often.

Similarly, as long as the firm operates, it needs to purchase storage. The idea that a firm can delay purchasing storage indefinitely by constantly increasing the utilization rate is, to put it bluntly, misinformed. The long-term key to financial success in terms of storage management is optimizing storage usage to minimize the frequency and magnitude of storage purchases. A high allocation efficiency rate helps decrease the size and number of storage purchases, as does a high utilization efficiency rate.

NOTE	Capacity on-demand programs are alternative procurement strategies aimed at alleviating the frequency and number of storage purchases. Although these "pay-as-you-go" methods are quite successful at easing the purchase and planning process, they do little to address the rate of consumption or poor utilization found in many environments.

Utilization Efficiency

There might be environments in which the allocation efficiency is at a desirable rate, but the allocated storage is misused, unusable, abandoned, or even hoarded. This is what Toigo refers to as poor utilization efficiency, whereby the storage itself might be highly allocated, but poorly utilized. In fact, in many open systems environments in which the storage capacity is efficiently allocated, utilization efficiency might be extremely poor, with many applications needlessly consuming data that is rarely, if ever, used.

To resolve these types of issues, a targeted program or project aimed at reclaiming allocated—but lost or poorly used storage—is needed. A project of this magnitude requires a significant time investment and an energetic executive sponsor who is capable of ensuring the proper alignment of goals and initiatives. A storage reclamation project also requires extensive use of a combination of off-the-shelf storage resource management (SRM) software and home-grown scripts dedicated to tracking storage consumption.

Despite the many obstacles that are known factors in implementing DAS, the majority of disk units sold in the last five years are still connected to hosts in a direct-attached fashion. Most companies—even early adopters of storage networking technologies—are still in the implementation phase of building SANs, and therefore have at least a partial mix of SAN and DAS technologies in the datacenter.

Although it is difficult to determine the exact percentage of DAS and SAN storage currently installed world-wide, estimates based on the sales of disk and Fibre Channel gear indicate that nearly three quarters of all disk storage units installed still utilize the direct-attached architecture. As shown in Table 1-1, DAS storage units made up nearly 70 percent of all storage sales in 2003 (with NAS and SAN storage together comprising approximately 30 percent). As these figures indicate, there is still a long way to go before the majority of storage environments currently deployed are networked storage solutions.

In addition to the recently installed DAS, a mountain of DAS that was purchased during the market upswing and it still carries a sizable net book value. As shown in Table 1-1, nearly one million DAS units were shipped between 2001 and 2003, indicating significant depreciation expense for customers when considering the corresponding low utilization rate (and the high COPQ) for DAS.

Conclusion

Networked storage offers strategic benefits over DAS by providing significant cost advantages. Networked storage creates economies of scale and increases operational efficiencies, which reduce the TCO. Networked storage also provides the requisite technology for resolving many storage-related issues, such as the need for long distance data replication.

The current process of managing heterogeneous storage on a storage network is a complex one that at this point in time diminishes operational economies of scale. As storage management software matures, however, operational efficiencies related to managing heterogeneous storage will increase and the TCO for heterogeneous storage will decrease.

Utilizing a tiered storage infrastructure allows more granular management of costs associated with storage management and will in the future (as storage management software matures) lower the overall TCO for storage.

If the charge is then for the CIO to provide the following conditions, then a prime area of concentration for IT departments should be to enable a storage vision that addresses the firm's storage vulnerabilities:

- Scalable, cost-efficient storage solutions that increase the availability of mission-critical business information

- Sound recoverability to business operations in the event of a disaster

- Flexible environments that increase productivity through increased uptime

- Increased business value via cost avoidance and the decreased frequency of hardware procurements through increased yield

A storage vision begins with the consolidation and decommissioning of DAS (and its migration to a networked storage infrastructure) and ends with a framework of cost-effective, tiered storage solutions that are tailored to support applications with storage as a utility-like service.

Summary

This chapter discussed how the commoditization of storage hardware and the poor utilization rates endemic to DAS environments lead to poor storage yield, a correspondingly high COPQ, and an increased TCO for storage. Storage networks provide strategic advantages by lowering IT costs and by eliminating the waste associated with poor storage utilization. Storage networks also address vulnerabilities by increasing data availability.

In the following chapter, I outline how the tangible and intangible benefits of networked storage, primarily increased utilization and increased availability, can lead to a reduction in the TCO for storage.

End Notes

[1] Reprinted by permission of *Harvard Business Review*. From "IT Doesn't Matter" by Nicholas Carr, May 2003. Copyright 2003 by the Harvard Business School Publishing Corporation; all rights reserved.

[2] From "Does IT Matter? Information Technology and the Corrosion of Competitive Advantage" by Nicholas Carr, 2004. Copyright 2004 by the Harvard Business School Publishing Corporation; all rights reserved.

[3] From "How Competitive Forces Shape Strategy" by Michael E. Porter. *Harvard Business Review* March/April, 1979. Copyright 1979 by Harvard Business School Publishing; all rights reserved.

[4] IDC 2004. Framingham, MA.

—"Worldwide Disk Storage Systems, 2003-2008 Market Forecast and Analysis: Conservatism Persists, but Opportunities Abound," IDC #31663, forthcoming.

—"Worldwide Disk Storage Systems Forecast and Analysis," 2003-2007, IDC #30247, October 2003.

—"Worldwide Disk Storage Systems Forecast and Analysis," 2002-2006, IDC #28261, December 2002.

[5] Toigo, Jon William. "The Holy Grail of Data Storage Management," Upper Saddle River, New Jersey: Prentice-Hall PTR, 2000.

[6] Greenspan, Alan. "The Challenge of Central Banking in a Democratic Society," Annual Dinner and Francis Boyer Lecture of The American Enterprise Institute for Public Policy Research, Washington, D.C. December 5, 1996. Accessed July 6, 2004, http://www.federalreserve.gov/BOARDDOCS/SPEECHES/19961205.htm.

[7] IDC, 2004.

—"Worldwide Disk Storage Systems 2003-2008 Market Forecast and Analysis: Conservatism Persists, but Opportunities Abound," IDC #31663, forthcoming.

—"Worldwide Disk Storage Systems Forecast and Analysis," 2003-2007, IDC #30247, October 2003.

—"Worldwide Disk Storage Systems Forecast and Analysis," 2002-2006, IDC #28261, December 2002.

[8] Berinato, Scott. "What Went Wong at Cisco?" *CIO Magazine*, August, 2001.

[9] The Bureau of Economic Analysis at the U.S. Department of Commerce tracks the U.S. Gross Domestic Product by analyzing a series of major accounts of U.S. goods. The most up-to-date analysis can be found on the BEA website at http://www.bea.doc.gov/.

[10] McKinsey Global Institute, "US Productivity Growth 1995-2000: Understanding the Contribution of Information Technology Relative to Other Factors." Washington, D.C.: McKinsey & Company, October 2001.

[11] National Bureau of Economic Research, Business Cycle Dating Committee. "The NBER's Recession Dating Procedure," October 21, 2003. Accessed, July 17, 2003, http://www.nber.org/cycles/recessions.html.

[12] DeLong, Summers, "The 'New Economy': Background, Historical Perspective, Questions, and Speculations." *Federal Reserve Bank of Kansas City, Economic Review*, Fourth Quarter, 2001.

[13] ibid.

[14] EMC Corporation. Form 10-K, Annual report for the fiscal year ended: December 31, 2002. Retrieved June 3, 2004 from EDGAR.

[15] EMC Corporation. Form 10-K, Annual report for the fiscal year ended: December 31, 2003. Retrieved June 28, 2004 from EDGAR. Form 10 K, Annual report for the fiscal year ended: December 31, 2002. Retrieved June 3, 2004 from EDGAR.

[16] IDC. Framingham, MA.

—"Worldwide Fibre Channel Host Bus Adapter 2004-2008 Forecast and 2003 Vendor Shares," IDC #30925, March 2004.

—"Worldwide Fibre Channel Host Bus Adapter Forecast and Analysis, 2003-2007," IDC #29414, May 2003.

—"Worldwide Fibre Channel Switch 2004-2008 Forecast and 2003 Vendor Shares," IDC #31362, June 2004.

—"Worldwide Fibre Channel Hub and Switch Forecast and Analysis, 2003-2007," IDC #29882, August 2003.

[17] IDC. Framingham, MA. 2004. Source: IDC Worldwide Quarterly Server Tracker, Q1 2004 release.

[18] IDC. Framingham, MA. 2004.

—"Worldwide Disk Storage Systems 2003-2008 Market Forecast and Analysis: Conservatism Persists, but Opportunities Abound," IDC #31663, forthcoming.

—"Worldwide Storage Software Forecast and Analysis, 2003-2007," IDC #29983, August 2003.

—"Worldwide Storage Software Forecast and Analysis, 2002-2006," IDC #27477, June 2002.

—"Worldwide and U.S. Storage Services 2004-2008 Forecast: The Opportunity Shifts," IDC #31042, March 2004.

—"Worldwide and U.S. Storage Services Forecast and Analysis, 2003-2007," IDC #28992, March 2003.

[19] U.S. Census Bureau. "Retail 2Q, 2003 E-Commerce Report," http://www.census.gov/mrts/www/current.html. August 22, 2003. Retrieved September 2003.

[20] U.S. Census Bureau. "Retail 1Q, 2004 E-Commerce Report," http://www.census.gov/mrts/www/current.html. May 21, 2004. Retrieved August 2004.

[21] U.S. Census Bureau. "United States Department of Commerce E-Stats," March 19 2003, http://www.census.gov/estats. Retrieved September 2003.

[22] Securities Exchange Commission. "Interagency Concept Release: Draft Interagency White Paper on Sound Practices to Strengthen the Resilience of the U. S. Financial System; Rel. No. 34-46432." Retrieved August 2003. SEC. August 2002. http://www.sec.gov/rules/concept/34-46432.htm.

[23] Ibid.

[24] Securities Exchange Commission. "Interagency Paper on Sound Practices to Strengthen the Resilience of the U.S. Financial System; Release No. 34-47638," http://www.sec.gov/news/studies/34-47638.htm. Retrieved August 2003. SEC. August 2002.

[25] Securities Exchange Commission. "SEC News Digest, Enforcement Proceedings," http://www.sec.gov/news/digest/12-03.txt Retrieved August 2003. SEC. December 3 2002.

[26] There are reams of quality management and Six-Sigma resources available on the web but a good basic definition of COPQ can be found here: http://software.isixsigma.com/dictionary/Cost_of_Poor_Quality-63.htm

[27] Christian Terwiesch, Roger E. Bohn, "The Economics of Yield Driven Processes," Working Paper, Wharton Operations and Information Management Department, The Wharton School, 1998.

[28] Toigo Partners International, LLC. "Storage Management 2003: "The 'Two Towers' of Storage Pain Part One: Provisioning," Toigo Partners International, LLC. 2003: pp2–3.

[29] Merrill Lynch, McKinsey & Company. "The Storage Report – Customer Perspectives & Industry Evolution," Merrill Lynch, McKinsey & Company, June 19, 2001: p 40.

[30] Moore, Fred. "Horison Information Strategies: Storage Facts, Figures, Estimates, and Rules of Thumb," Copyright Fred Moore, 2003.

CHAPTER 2

THE BUSINESS IMPACT OF STORAGE NETWORKING TECHNOLOGY

The previous chapter discussed the strategic nature of IT solutions, gave a brief economic history of the last five years, and demonstrated how issues such as poor utilization have plagued companies with large, direct-attached storage (DAS) installations.

This chapter presents the tangible and intangible benefits of storage networks, and evaluates each storage networking technology solution within the context of meeting today's demanding business requirements.

Additionally it discusses in detail the measurement of the total cost of ownership (TCO) for storage solutions (this is the most critical piece of financial analysis), and it demonstrates the basic steps required to build a TCO model for storage. Understanding the financial impact of storage networks is crucial to presenting the business case to management and it is a fundamental step in ensuring that your project meets its financial goals as planned.

This chapter covers the following topics:

- Tangible and intangible benefits of storage networking

- Technology solutions associated with storage networking

- Increased availability

- Backup and recovery options

- Replication

- SAN extensions

- Total cost of ownership (TCO)

Tangible and Intangible Benefits of Storage Networking

The networking of data storage arose from needs similar to those that drove the adoption of local-area networks (LANs). LANs are a technical solution to the functional problem of users being unable to share resources. The need to share files, printers, and compute cycles accelerated the advent of the LAN and its widespread adoption in corporations and universities. Likewise, the requirement to logically combine and physically share groups of disks between servers and across business functions has driven the adoption of storage area networks (SANs).

The ability to share relatively expensive disks across multiple resources to share and drive down operational costs has helped to build the business case for deploying SAN storage. This is not to say that deploying SAN storage—an innately complex and labor-intensive exercise—is without its own set of difficulties; however, the value achieved from doing so is significant.

One fundamental difference between the early days of Ethernet networking and the recent advances in storage networking is that when Ethernet began, there was a concerted focus among vendors to ensure that data communications were facilitated using commonly agreed upon standards. Because of the open systems nature of the solution, data transmission would ultimately fail if certain precepts were not fully agreed upon during implementation.

As far as storage networking is concerned, however, few standards with the exception of basic connectivity protocols have been mutually accepted; therefore, the tendency is for customers to implement isolated homogeneous storage networking islands based on vendor-specific solutions.

As seen in Chapter 1, "Industry Landscape: Storage Costs and Consumption," the sheer numbers of direct-attached environments that are potential candidates for migrations to SANs present a serious management headache to IT storage teams if the environments themselves are to remain homogeneous (not to mention a huge financial boon to a select few hardware vendors). Interoperability has historically been low on the list of vendor initiatives, with a large portion of disk arrays shipping without a management interface or an SNMP Management Information Base (MIBs). This is partially due to the tremendous amount of work that is required to redo or modify data schemas and MIBs . It is also safe to assume that while the storage market was booming, there was little justification for storage vendors to provide mechanisms that would enable better management of storage devices. Disk and Fibre Channel switch vendors recently made inroads with manageability by opening their APIs, or at least sharing them to some degree with software developers, although many are still behind the customer demand curve as far as producing software tools that provide the exact desired functionality when it comes to management of storage devices.

Interoperability continues to be an issue for the immediate future, but there are still financial benefits to implementing networked storage solutions. As shown in Chapter 1, the issue of utilization is the primary cost factor with DAS. From a fiscal standpoint, it is possible to increase storage allocation efficiency 5 percent to 40 percent just by using Fibre Channel switches as dumb hubs. The additional port capacity drives the per MB and per port costs up only marginally, but it allows administrators to access the remaining stranded storage, thereby increasing utilization. The addition of Fibre Channel switches to DAS environments and the use of storage networking technologies increases the allocation efficiency (the metric normally known as utilization) and can therefore eliminate the cost of poor quality (COPQ) associated with DAS environments.

You see later in this chapter how the COPQ contributes to the firm's TCO for storage.

Of course, the addition of the Fibre Channel switch to the environment adds a measure of complexity, additional labor costs, and an incremental hardware cost to the TCO for this environment. Depending on the skills of the team supporting the switch hardware, the increased training costs or increased costs from consulting or temporary headcount might be significant.

Also keep in mind that the addition of Fibre Channel switch hardware and the creation of a SAN does nothing to intrinsically increase the utilization efficiency (the way applications use the storage they've been allocated) of the environment. Ultimately, improving the way applications utilize storage is the best way to increase storage utilization efficiencies.

NOTE Chapter 1 mentioned the creation of a storage recovery program dedicated to the analysis of application utilization trends. As part of the storage program, subject matter experts should have an analysis of table spaces and data usage trends as their charter. Attention to these details should ensure that the application's requirements match the storage solutions deployed and that the applications themselves appropriately use the storage allocated to them.

In addition to a storage recovery program, a storage consolidation program assists in increasing the financial benefits of a Fibre Channel environment. The migration from DAS to SAN storage paves the way for storage consolidation. Many DAS environments— especially those in which the disk units near the end of their depreciation cycle—have smaller disk drives (typically 36 GB,

18 GB, or even 9 GB). 73 GB, 146 GB, and 181 GB disk drives are capable of rotational speeds equal to or superior to that of the smaller drives and the increased capacity in a single footprint easily justifies consolidation. A consolidation project can also alleviate hardware and software maintenance bills by facilitating the decommissioning of older, smaller capacity disk storage units.

The implementation of a SAN framework, when coupled with a consolidation effort, can lead to collapsed points of management, which alleviates some labor costs and releases precious datacenter space.

Technology Solutions Associated with Storage Networking

There is no magic bullet when it comes to implementing a storage networking architecture. Moving from DAS to SAN requires restructuring your environment on a grand scale. At a fundamental level, there is resistance when putting another device in the data path between the host and the storage. In addition to cultural changes regarding support models, there are perceived issues and real issues with regard to performance that need to be addressed. In addition, physical requirements, such as cabling, are often ignored until the last minute, which can produce serious headaches when it is time for implementation and rollout.

In summary, implementing a SAN means work. As pessimistic as this might sound, however, all is not lost. In addition to the financial ramifications of increasing the storage allocation efficiency, the reclamation of datacenter space, and the reduction of hardware maintenance bills through consolidation (all efforts that require more work), SANs do have intrinsic, tangible benefits.

Increased Availability

Increased port capacity and redundancy are popular features of Fibre Channel SANs. The elimination of a single point of failure in the host-storage relationship is significant and increases business availability and uptime. Figure 2-1 illustrates the concept of a single point of failure on an application in a DAS environment.

Figure 2-1   *Sample DAS Configuration*

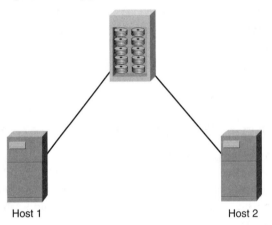

Host 1   Host 2

In Figure 2-1, two non-clustered hosts share a single storage frame without the benefit of a SAN. If the application residing on Host 1 is not mirrored on Host 2, and the link between Host 1 and the storage array is dropped, then the application cannot access its storage. There is no way for the disk devices attached to Host 1 to be shared with Host 2; therefore, the application on Host 1 is prevented from starting on Host 2. Similarly, if Host 1 goes down, there is no way to bring up the application from Host 1 on Host 2. This *many-to-one* configuration does not offer high availability or data resiliency.

Figure 2-2 shows the elimination of the single point of failure in the same environment with the installation of two 16-port Fibre Channel fabric switches and the creation of a SAN.

Figure 2-2   *SAN Configuration Examples*

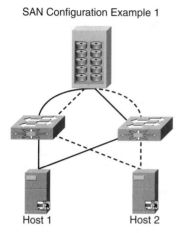

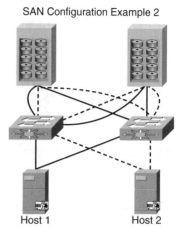

In Example 1 of Figure 2-2, both Host 1 and Host 2 have multiple paths to the disk through two fixed 16-port Fibre Channel switches. The multiple paths through the Fibre Channel switches create redundancy. In the event of a loss of one of the Fibre Channel links, the applications on Host 1 and Host 2 can still access storage over the SAN. Additionally, this configuration supports what is called a *poor man's cluster*. In other words, if the applications are mirrored (via content management software or via a manual file synchronization process) across both Host 1 and Host 2, and one of the hosts goes offline, the remaining host can (using volume management software) import the disk groups normally reserved for the other host and successfully bring the application back online. There is still the issue of the storage unit as a single point of failure, an issue that can be addressed with multiple, redundant storage units and more frequent backups.

In Example 2 of Figure 2-2, all single points of failure have been eliminated. If clustering is enabled at the host and application level, both hosts should be able to access storage as long as the appropriate volume and logical unit number (LUN) management software is enabled and properly configured. This *any-to-any* relationship is one of the key benefits of implementing SAN technology.

The financial impact of mission-critical application downtime cannot be overstated. Based on data from the U.S. Department of Commerce Census Bureau, recent estimates of e-commerce retail sales for the second quarter of 2004 were $15.7 billion.[1] This figure works out to roughly $121,141.98 per minute of downtime or $2,019.03 per second—not a trivial amount of money. These numbers highlight the well-known fact that availability affects revenue.

Backup and Recovery Options

One fundamental benefit of networking storage devices is the positive implications for backup strategies. In addition to sharing backup resources, such as tape libraries and SANs, coupled with the advent of *serial advanced technology attachment* (SATA) disk drives and *snap* technologies, enable the creation of highly customized backup and recovery strategies that offer the business increased availability and uptime are less difficult and less expensive to implement.

LAN-Free Backups

The ability to share storage devices creates economies of scale and lowers the TCO for backup solutions. Previous to the advent of SAN storage, tape devices and libraries were either configured in a one-to-one fashion or shared over an IP-based network via a media server, adding extra management complexity and extra hardware costs to the backup solution. LAN-free backups, on the other hand, move the backup traffic to the Fibre Channel network, thereby freeing up IP capacity on the LAN and boosting backup and restore performance.

LAN-based and LAN-free backups are shown in Figure 2-3. In the example on the left, all backup traffic from the hosts to the backup servers traverses the IP network before going to tape. In the example on the right, the backup traffic traverses only the private Fibre Channel fabric, avoiding the utilization of the IP network infrastructure. The additional Fibre Channel array in the LAN-free backup example can be used for multiple staged copies of data and for software-based disk-to-disk or server-free backups, an example of which we discuss next.

Figure 2-3   *LAN-Based and LAN-Free Backups*

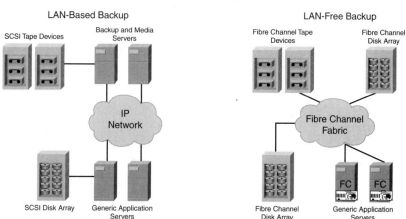

Server-Free Backups

The utilization of SAN infrastructure allows environments to eliminate the need for sending data over the wire to a backup or media server. In essence, server-free or disk-to-disk backups obviate both the extra overhead involved with backup and media server infrastructures, lowering the labor and management costs involved with tape backups, and increase the capability of an environment to meet its recovery time objective (RTO). Recovery from tape is often not a viable solution for large, mission-critical environments because restoring a 1-TB database from tape generally means the application must be offline for most of a day. This is not to say that tape backups do not have a place. For audit purposes, government regulations stipulate data retention of up to seven years for some financial data sets. For environments in which restores are not time-sensitive, a tape copy is a cost-effective solution. Where time is of the essence and RTOs are measured in minutes, a disk-to-disk backup solution is required. Disk-to-disk backup solutions are not new; EMC's TimeFinder has been used extensively in Small Computer Systems Interface (SCSI) environments for some time. Hitachi System's True Copy and Hewlett Packard's Business Copy are similar products offering similar services. Fibre Channel fabrics, however, offer performance increases over SCSI and enable the same many-to-many relationships, as shown previously in the LAN-free backups. Coupling these infrastructure advantages with disk copy solutions brings great economies of scale to the backup arena.

An additional benefit of disk-to-disk backups is the capability to share multiple copies of data between environments over the Fibre Channel fabric. For example, using "snap" technologies, multiple copies of databases and code trees can be shared change to among all hosts on the Fibre Channel fabric, eliminating the need for manual copies of separate environments. Snapshots are also commonly associated with network-attached storage (NAS) devices. Figure 2-4 shows a basic example of a disk-to-disk backup solution.

Figure 2-4 *Disk-to-Disk Backup*

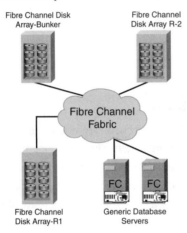

In the example in Figure 2-4, the database servers access the primary copy of data (R1) residing on the external disk through the Fibre Channel fabric. Disk-to-disk backup can then take place over the Fibre Channel fabric to the R2 copy on the secondary Fibre Channel array. Multiple copies of the data can be stored on the third Fibre Channel array—the bunker frame—depending on application availability requirements and RTOs. For highest availability, the data can be copied multiple times a day from the R1 to the R2 and then staged on the bunker frame, offering point-in-time recovery options that match business requirements. For environments that require shared data, other groups of hosts can utilize the R2 copies without performance impact to either the host or the R1 copy by merely attaching to the SAN fabric.

Replication

Replication of data has long been a key factor in most companies' plans for disaster recovery. A key trait of replication is that it has never been easy to do, and like many other storage management solutions, products that could perform to customers' needs were, until recently, difficult to come by. In many cases, instead of a packaged software solution, what is used for long-distance replication is a conglomeration of homegrown scripts designed to preserve, manage, and copy transaction logs from a primary site to a second (or third) geographically-remote site at the time the logs are applied to a waiting database. This solution, although primitive (it is subject to QoS constraints on the IP networking framework and prone to human error) has worked well for many customers in lieu of commercially available solutions.

Asynchronous Replication

The manual process of copying and applying logs is a form of asynchronous replication, whereby the two data sets are not kept completely in sync, but are synchronized during a period or periods of batch processing. Software solutions provided by external disk vendors and specifically designed to manage disk-to-disk copies asynchronously between locations are able to ensure, through discrete algorithms, that the data is staged in the proper order as it arrives, with minimal impact to the application or to the IP backbone. The benefits of asynchronous replication are clear: less consumption of network bandwidth and less impact on the performance of the remote application. The disadvantage of asynchronous replication should be obvious in terms of business continuance: If the business is impacted by a catastrophic failure or natural disaster, there is a window of opportunity during which the data is not synchronized with production.

Synchronous Replication

Synchronous replication is ideal for environments in which little or no downtime is acceptable in the event of an outage. Cutover to the secondary or disaster recovery environment should be transparent to the end user or occur within seconds at the most. Geoclustering, or live mirroring between remote sites, is appropriate for customers who cannot lose a single transaction or cannot tolerate an outage window of more than a few seconds. Customers in the financial sector are, as demonstrated in Chapter 1, likely candidates for these types of solutions. The obvious disadvantage of synchronous replication is the possibility of latency. Given the intolerance for latency built into most databases and applications, synchronous replication is typically performed over an optical network to minimize delay.

During synchronous replication, writes are acknowledged only when the data from the source is updated at the target. Therefore, in some cases, synchronous data replication might not be an ideal solution for long distances, without the use of traffic management techniques such as QoS to maintain performance, which can increase the complexity of the solution and the amount of hands-on management required. Synchronous replication is, however, the best way to ensure that the production and the disaster recovery copies are kept updated as of the last transaction.

Disaster recovery planners who work with applications that are more tolerant of latency or delay might find significant ROI in architecting disaster recovery environments based on IP storage, the primary advantage of which is dispensing with the distance limitations of native or dark fiber.

Both types of replication can take place via software-only solutions (such as those manufactured by Topio or Alacritus) or over additional out-of-band appliances (such as those manufactured by Kashya). This type of technology is often referred to as *continuous data protection* or just *data protection*. Replication traffic can be carried over SAN extensions or for shorter distances over native fiber.

Fibre Channel SANs not only allow sharing of storage devices between logical groups of hosts, but the nature of fiber-based transport is such that it can carry high-speed (up to 2125 Mbps) data over long-distances (up to 10 KM unassisted) to extend the physical footprint of SANs and link datacenters for the purposes of disaster recovery and data sharing. Figure 2-5 demonstrates linking two datacenters via a single Fibre Channel SAN fabric.

Figure 2-5   *Virtual Datacenter via Fibre Channel SAN Fabric*

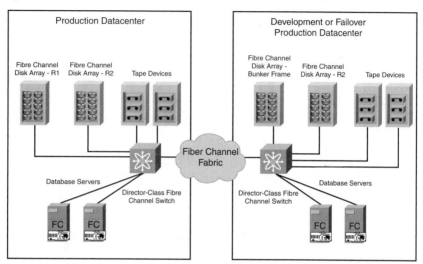

In the example in Figure 2-5, a development and a production datacenter are linked together over a single Fibre Channel fabric. Two director class switches act as *gateways* between each datacenter. For increased availability, (assuming that multiple, redundant fiber runs are available between each location), these switches can be augmented with an additional pair of director class switches at both sites. The previous example creates a *virtual datacenter* via native Fibre Channel, and it extends the any-to-any model up to 10KM.

SAN Extensions

Extending SANs over longer distances is crucial for optimal business continuance and might be required, as industry regulations or government legislation show. To increase the distance between storage networks, the following technologies might be implemented depending on budget allocations and the infrastructure and capacity already in place:

- Optical networking

- Fibre Channel over Internet Protocol (FCIP)

- Internet Fibre Channel Protocol (iFCP)
- Internet SCSI (iSCSI)

Optical Networking

Optical networks are instrumental in carrying data over long distances. Metropolitan-area networks (MANs) and long-haul networks typically utilize an optical backbone via synchronous optical network/synchronous digital hierarchy (SONET/SDH) or asynchronous transfer mode (ATM). IP over SONET (Packet over SONET [PoS]) has grown in popularity and is increasingly used in applications traditionally reserved for ATM, although it is a long way from replacing ATM entirely.

Dense wave division multiplexing (DWDM) and coarse wave division multiplexing (CWDM) are methods of boosting capacity of the physical fiber layer by coalescing (multiplexing) multiple laser wavelengths onto the same fiber. Increasingly, DWDM and CWDM are used to maximize available bandwidth for applications and environments that require increased availability and uptime.

DWDM and CWDM both support Enterprise Systems Connection (ESCON), Fibre Connection (FICON), and Fibre Channel (FC), but historically, optical networking has been cost prohibitive for deployment within smaller institutions. Although DWDM and CWDM are not equal in terms of capacity and throughput, the differences in cost (CWDM is significantly cheaper than DWDM) can lead to wider deployment of CWDM as a backbone for extending SANs.

Other low-cost alternatives for carrying storage traffic long distances and linking SANs are making inroads with enterprises that seek the full range of data protection available by replicating and sharing data to remote sites.

Fibre Channel over Internet Protocol

FCIP acts as a bridge between two independent SANs by encapsulating FC traffic into IP packets and pushing that data through an IP tunnel. Although there are no physical distance limitations, depending on the capacity of the current IP networking infrastructure, jitter and latency can occur over longer distances. Many organizations already have ample IP networking capacity in place to support some usage models; however, depending on the speed of the network connection, live mirroring, remote clustering, or synchronous (or asynchronous over slower links) replication might not be appropriate. For example, FCIP might be appropriate in the storage service provider space, but overkill on a small campus that can be serviced over native, dark fiber.

Figure 2-6 highlights the simplicity and the versatility of FCIP. Joining FC SANs over an IP network using a multiprotocol SAN switch provides long distance replication capabilities while sharing resources over disparate geographies.

Figure 2-6   *FCIP Usage*

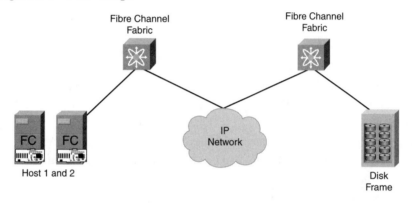

Internet Fibre Channel Protocol

Whereas FCIP is typically hosted over a card on a Fibre Channel switch, iFCP works through a separate gateway device on a network to wrap FC traffic in IP packet format. iFCP gives Fibre Channel devices IP addresses so that the FC devices appear to run native IP. This allows FC devices and FC traffic to be routable (and manageable through network monitoring tools). Like FCIP, there are no physical distance limitations, and iFCP utilizes existing IP and FC resources, specifically, Internet routers and switches and FC HBAs (host bus adapters). iFCP relies on iSNS (Internet Storage Name Server), as does iSCSI, to provide network address and device name resolution. Figure 2-7 shows an iFCP topology with iFCP gateways carrying Fibre Channel traffic on an IP network.

Figure 2-7 *iFCP Gateway*

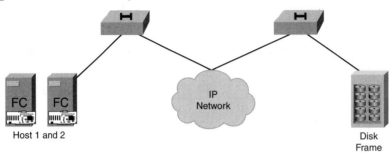

Internet SCSI

Internet SCSI (iSCSI) is a protocol designed to encapsulate SCSI commands within IP packets, allowing SCSI traffic to be routed and managed like any other IP packet. Much of iSCSI's adoption thus far can be attributed to its low TCO. The fact that iSCSI leverages existing IP or Gigabit Ethernet and DAS resources makes it an excellent fit for environments that have a high percentage of DAS storage, little investment in Fibre Channel, and less stringent performance requirements for long-distance data replication. iSCSI is often not a good match for high performance and high availability scenarios, such as live mirroring or synchronous replication of databases over long distances; however, iSCSI can be used to mirror or replicate other data types (file and print sharing) to remote locations in a cost-effective fashion. iSCSI can be utilized over existing network interface cards or cards known as TCP Offload Engines (TOE cards), which partially or fully alleviate the burden of sharing client IP traffic over the same pipe as what is used for SCSI data.

iSCSI environments can be configured to run over a separate iSCSI router, as illustrated in Figure 2-8, or over an iSCSI blade in a multi-protocol SAN switch.

Figure 2-8 *Typical iSCSI Installation*

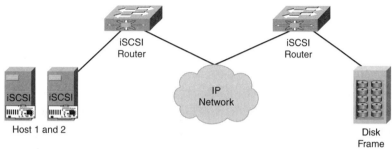

IP storage networks are poised for mass adoption. IP is a fully-evolved standard and most corporate environments have already adopted IP technology on a wide scale. The wholesale adoption of IP networking means that security and monitoring tools are already IP-aware and networking talents are well versed in IP management best practices. Many NAS devices on the market today ship with support for iSCSI and many other vendors have conceded to the IP storage paradigm. As the standards for FCIP and IFCP become hardened, companies will rush to establish their presence in those markets and more products will become widely available.

Given the number and type of solutions available on the market, evaluating the solution and matching the appropriate technology to each individual environment is critical. When the appropriate technology is selected and a value is assigned to the solution, it becomes possible to match the solution to the right tier.

To select the appropriate technology, it is necessary to first define the problem (availability, replication, and so on). It is then necessary to look at the TCO for each solution and compare the projected impact of each solution using generally accepted financial metrics. Select the appropriate solution using one or more of the metrics covered in Chapter 3, "Building a Value Case Using Financial Metrics," based on your company's methodology for benchmarking the financial impact of new projects.

Total Cost of Ownership

TCO analysis—although it is painstaking and time-consuming—is the only way to provide the level of detail and coverage required to help business stakeholders understand the impact of using technology. TCO analysis counters the reigning perception that resources are, because of economies of scale and purchasing power, free. Looking at the TCO of a solution is the only way to understand the impact of using or implementing a technology solution. Ultimately, having an accurate TCO number for storage is the only way to determine the ROI from increased utilization and is a fundamental requirement for creating the tiered storage model. Having an up-to-date storage TCO requires significant effort and ongoing analysis, but it is well worth the effort.

A functional TCO for storage reflects all aspects of the costs of implementing a storage solution including all hard and soft costs associated with a product implementation from purchase to deployment and finally decommission. Also known as fully-burdened costs, after it is determined, TCO is a cold, hard kernel of financial truth that reflects the true financial impact of the resources tied up in an environment.

Here is a brief example. The Goodrich IT department decides that to justify decommissioning a duplicate development environment, they need to provide a TCO metric that demonstrates the significant costs associated with the environment.

The team does some fairly intensive research that produces the following data. Keep in mind that the capital costs for the storage frame and the tape library are depreciated:

- The 3.5 TB of storage attached to the frame was purchased two years ago for $350,000 (the frame still has one year of depreciation remaining).

- The frame has an annual hardware and software maintenance contract of $100,000.

- The datacenter support team has analyzed the cost for providing and supporting one square foot tile of datacenter space, and it determined the cost to be $10,000 per year.

- The footprint of the frame itself is 1.5 feet and the frame consumes 1/100 of the power and cooling cost of the datacenter, which comes to $50,000 per month.

- The development environment is backed up once a week to its own dedicated tape library, which was purchased at the same time as the frame for $250,000.

- Goodrich pays $50,000 a year for tape cartridges and offsite storage of tapes for this datacenter. This development environment consumes 1/25 of this resource.

- Neither the frame nor the library is attached to a SAN. The frame and the library are only 60 percent allocated with all ports in use.

- The storage support team is comprised of two full-time employees; each earns $75,000 annually. They spend 50 percent of their time supporting this development environment.

NOTE   As mentioned earlier, the COPQ and allocation efficiency contribute significantly to the TCO.

Table 2-1 recaps the associated costs.

Table 2-1   *TCO Analysis*

Goodrich IT Data	Value
Total Storage	3,584,000 MB
Allocation Efficiency	60%
Allocated Storage	2,150,400 MB
Frame Purchase Price	$350,000
Frame Depreciation Expense	$116,667
Hardware/Software Maintenance	$100,000
Data Center Utilization	$15,000
Facilities Expense	$6000
Tape Library	$250,000
Tape Library Depreciation Expense	$83,333.33
Backup Expense	$2000
Labor	$75,000
Total Costs	$398,000
Total Costs per MB	$0.19

The application team currently using the development environment claims that the storage is an insignificant cost—only $0.10 per MB, based on its purchase price. Given the calculations outlined in Table 2-1, however, the IT department (specifically, the storage support team) is able to counter with a highly detailed analysis of the annualized costs of the storage in this environment. The fully burdened costs are almost twice what the application team claims. The application team is now able to understand that instead of consuming a purchased asset of $0.10 per MB, the environment actually costs $0.19 per MB for every year it is in use, or $0.56 per MB for the life of the solution.

The two key elements of TCO analysis are annualizing all related costs and then resolving those costs on a cost per MB basis. TCO analysis clearly requires significant effort, even more so when evaluating the costs across an entire enterprise.

NOTE   A note about head count and utilization. Head count costs are typically not just annualized salary, but are also medical and life insurance and benefits including bonuses and training expenses. The human resources department at your firm likely has a dollar figure associated with each employee in a salary band, and chances are it is significantly higher than the employee's base salary. For the Goodrich example, it is reasonable to assume that the actual labor cost for an employee is in excess of $100,000.

NOTE   Utilization efficiency rates, as discussed in Chapter 1, are not easy figures to come by. Analysis of the environment from the application level to the physical allocation level (using SRM tools and home-grown scripts) is required to get a true picture of both allocation utilization and utilization efficiency. These numbers, when taken together, provide a better picture of the storage TCO. For the purposes of this example, if the allocation rate is 60 percent, but the utilization efficiency is only 30 percent, the annual TCO for the storage in this environment is actually $0.37, or almost quadruple the cost estimates from the application team!

One other caveat to remember when determining the TCO for storage in an enterprise is that costs fluctuate over time and that solutions at different tiers have different cost structures. Obviously storage costs have decreased drastically over time, but the costs of labor and facilities also vary. Most costs typically decline over time and there needs to be some consideration for the decreasing costs, especially if the IT department or storage infrastructure teams plan to utilize a cost recovery or charge-back model for funding services. Fully burdened costs are required to facilitate the move to alternative funding models and the move to tiered storage; however, these costs must be accurate to avoid both overcharging the client as well as ending up short of funds.

Even though it can be painful, the math behind TCO is relatively simple, and although this example is a simplified overview of the elements involved with calculating TCO, TCO analysis is on the whole relatively straightforward.

Now is probably a good time to take a quick breather before going back for more. Thus far, I have given a brief overview of storage networking technologies and their most common usage scenarios. In addition, I broached the topic of TCO.

Now armed with both an overview of the storage networking technologies and a cursory understanding of how TCO analysis works, we can move on to the spicier materials behind financial metrics in Chapter 3.

Conclusion

The first step in building the business case for storage networks is finding the current TCO. Even if this number is only an approximation, it serves as a crucial piece of the calculations necessary to build the business case for implementing a storage vision based on networked storage strategies. The financial metrics outlined in Chapter 3 (with the exception of the payback method) use the TCO number to measure the impact of storage strategies, which in turn facilitates the creation of a solid business case for the use of networked storage.

End Notes

[1]United States Department of Commerce, http://www.census.gov/mrts/www/current.html.

BUILDING A VALUE CASE USING FINANCIAL METRICS

Understanding the financial impact of deploying an IT solution is the most critical part of the decision-making process. Projects involving the deployment of storage networks tend to be unique because the financial benefits associated with them (primarily increased utilization) are easily quantifiable, as demonstrated in Chapter 1, "Industry Landscape: Storage Costs and Consumption," and Chapter 2, "The Business Impact of Storage Networking Technology." Many IT projects—especially the ones designed to increase operational efficiencies—have benefits that are less easily measured, which makes building the value case for them more difficult.

Presenting an articulate, financially sound business case to management is a fundamental step in ensuring that your project is approved. Performing the analysis ahead of time, using proven financial metrics, and demonstrating the benefits of the project in a value case that supports the decision builds credibility not only in the project, but also in the project's leadership capabilities.

Value case analysis is not new; it has long been used to build decision matrices for corporations investing in real estate, manufacturing equipment, and mergers and acquisitions. It is used for any project in which significant investment is required. In recent history, value case analysis was often overlooked when it came to IT investments; however, given the recent economic climate and the increased attention to corporate governance, it is highly unlikely that large capital investments in IT can continue without highly detailed financial analyses to justify the expenditures.

It is critical that the project owner selects the appropriate metric based its relative merits and on his or her own company's methodology for benchmarking the financial impact of new projects. In this chapter, I cover in detail the following, most commonly used metrics:

- Payback method

- Return on Investment (ROI)

- Net Present Value (NPV)

- Economic Value Added (EVA)

- Value case analysis

Using Payback, ROI, NPV, and EVA

Budgeting and financial evaluation have always been, at least for most people, the most onerous parts of implementing a new technology. Unfortunately, planning and forecasting for projects involving new technology invariably involves a certain amount of black magic and there are risks everywhere: Will the product perform as expected? What does the vendor do if the product fails to perform adequately? What recourse is there if the product performs, but performs poorly? With tried-and-true products and solutions, the risk of poor product performance is minimized. With early adoption of new technologies, the risks are amplified.

A primary function of risk assessment and risk management is evaluating the impact of a technology solution on the firm's bottom line, and for new technologies, the importance of financial evaluation and value-case analysis is even more critical.

Just as choosing the right technology solution is critical for meeting business requirements, choosing the right methodology for valuing the project is equally important. It is also important for the methods used to match those used by the rest of the firm. For example, if a project is measured by a *hurdle rate* (or a required rate of return) that differs from the overall hurdle rate for the rest of the firm, the project can be viewed as a success by its stakeholders, whereas the rest of the business might consider it a failure.

This chapter looks at four of the most common methods of evaluating the financial success of a project and the advantages and disadvantages of each one.

NOTE   A critical aspect of the following methods is that each is customarily used to justify new capital investments based on revenue-facing environments. Each metric measures the financial benefit (or negative impact) of an investment based either on increased cash flows (revenue enhancements) or cost avoidance (expense reductions). Wherever possible, I highlight the functionality of these tools to evaluate their effectiveness in the context of IT projects that might or might not directly impact revenue. For the sake of simplicity, cost avoidance benefits are treated the same as revenue enhancements.

Payback Method

The payback method is commonly used in many businesses to evaluate capital purchases of relatively insignificant amounts.. The primary reason for its popularity is its ease of use. You could perform the payback method of analysis on a cocktail napkin or even in your head, as demonstrated in the following example.

The Goodrich Ice Cream Factory wants to decrease lines and increase revenue at one of its satellite stores during long summer nights. They want to add a second cash register to do this. A new cash register costs $2500. The management team at Goodrich estimates (based on sophisticated regression analysis and complex weather-forecasting models) that adding the second cash register can increase revenues by $1000 in June, $2000 in July, and $1000 in August. The cash register investment then reaches full payback three quarters of the way through July. This purchase is easily justified using the payback method.

The payback method is just that simple. Its simplicity, however, comes at a cost. Imagine what happens when the management team at Goodrich uses this methodology to justify the capital costs of building a new ice cream plant. The payback method, because it does not account for the time value of money, is not the appropriate tool to use.

Using the payback method to evaluate large capital investments has two significant drawbacks. Both drawbacks involve time.

The primary concern with using payback for large investments is that it is designed to measure the impact of an investment over short time horizons, such as with the cash register investment in which payback is accomplished in terms of months. When measuring the payback for building a new plant, the time horizons are longer and payback might not occur for a number of years. When the time horizons for a project are drawn out over a long period of time, the time value of money must be taken into account. The payback method lacks this capability.

The second issue with using payback analysis is obvious if you consider what happens after payback is reached. What if the labor to operate the new cash register and associated costs, such as power and maintenance, are significant? What if the cash flows for the months following payback are negative? You cannot capture the subsequent impact of the investment after payback is reached.

At a basic level, the failure of the payback method to take into consideration business-critical requirements makes it an unsatisfactory choice for justifying large IT purchases, such as storage networks.

NOTE	The payback method is especially difficult to use for projects that are not directly revenue-enhancing. For example, it is awkward to use the payback method to justify the purchase of a new backup infrastructure because, as with projects designed to increase operational efficiencies, the financial benefits (cash inflows or cost avoidances) of a new backup infrastructure are often difficult to quantify.

Return on Investment

ROI analysis is well received across all industries and as such, ROI analysis is commonly used to justify investments in IT hardware and software. The ROI ratio is understood as the following:

ROI = (Sum of all Returns) – (Sum of all Investments) / (Sum of all Investments)

NOTE	Although it is generally assumed that period returns are annualized, ROI horizons can be shortened or lengthened to fit the timeframe of the project as needed. Such flexibility can lead to abuses of ROI analysis.

Here is an example of the common usage of ROI to justify a project. The management team at Goodrich Ice Cream Factory wants to implement a data warehouse to analyze taste trends in the process of marketing new flavors. The team sends out a request for information (RFI) to several vendors and selects a product. The product purchase and implementation costs are estimated (based on the vendor's proposal) at $750,000. The IT infrastructure at Goodrich also needs to be upgraded to support the data warehouse, and the team is required to purchase multiple disk frames to store over 20 terabytes (TB) of customer preference data in a storage area network. New servers, new disks, and installation services for the data warehouse project (the code name of the project is Waterfront) cost an additional $750,000.

The management team believes, based on data from the vendor, that the Waterfront project will increase total revenues by $1,500,000 in the first full year after the implementation (year one), and $250,000 in the two subsequent years. Not only does this project look good in terms of the payback method (payback occurs in the first year), but the ROI is also a decent 33.33 percent. Table 3-1 shows the projected cash flows for Waterfront.

Table 3-1   *Waterfront Cash Flows*

Year	Cash Flow (in 1000s of dollars)
Year 0	($1500)
Year 1	$1500
Year 2	$250
Year 3	$250

The ROI for the project is:

ROI = (Sum of all Returns) – (Sum of all Investments) / (Sum of all Investments)

ROI = ($2000 – $1500) / $1500

ROI = 33.33 percent

Generally speaking, if the ROI percentage is positive, the project is well received. If the ROI percentage is greater than a firm's hurdle-rate—the generally agreed-upon cutoff rate for new projects—the project is a must do. The Waterfront team is satisfied with the projections and outlines plans to commence work.

A junior member of the Goodrich staff, however, who is assigned to the Waterfront team at the last minute, skips the project kickoff meeting to revisit the proposal. She notices that the per seat licensing and software maintenance costs, which were waived for the first year of implementation, are a staggering $1,000,000 in the second year of implementation, and another $500,000 in the third year.

Table 3-2 shows the revised cash flows for the Waterfront project.

Table 3-2   *Revised Waterfront Cash Flows*

Year	Cash Flow (in 1000s of dollars)
Year 0	($1500)
Year 1	$1500
Year 2	$–1000 + 250
Year 3	$–500 + 250

The ROI for this project then is:

ROI = (Sum of all Returns) – (Sum of all Investments) / (Sum of all Investments)

ROI = ($500 – $1500) / $3000

ROI = -33.33 percent

A negative ROI is the last thing anyone on the Waterfront team wants to see. Based on this analysis, the Waterfront project is halted and the project team schedules an offsite meeting to reevaluate the plans.

Above all, the most important rule of thumb for ROI math is to ensure that *all* costs are included. In some circumstances, all of the returns are counted, but many of the costs are excluded.

Ignoring the future costs of implementation in years 2 and 3 is a $1.5 million dollar mistake. Not only were the licensing and maintenance costs erroneously dismissed, but there is probably a good chance that other additional costs were overlooked, such as training for employees and additional temporary labor required to meet deadlines. Total cost of ownership analysis might have prevented this egregious error, but it would not have addressed the question of the time value of money and the cost of capital.

ROI analysis ignores the time value of money. The value of one dollar in cash flow today is ultimately different from what it will be tomorrow (hopefully, tomorrow it is worth more). ROI analysis also ignores the firm's cost of capital; therefore, when using ROI, you cannot account for how much it costs a firm to invest its money.

NOTE	ROI analysis can be adjusted to account for the cost of capital using EVA, as demonstrated in the "Economic Value Added" section.

Because evaluations of technology solutions based solely on ROI ignore these questions, ROI analysis is often seen as just a marketing tool. As a rule of thumb, ROI analysis is beneficial; however, it can also be manipulated to suit spurious marketing agendas.

ROI analysis is a step up from simple payback analysis, but until the company includes in its financial models the cost of capital and the time value of money, value cases built solely on ROI should be subject to intense scrutiny. ROI analysis should be used in tandem with other financial metrics, such as NPV and EVA.

Net Present Value

NPV is a way of projecting the financial worth of a project over time. Firms use NPV to roll back the value of anticipated cash flows from the future to the present day. NPV helps managers and planners understand the impact of choosing to do a certain project based on projected cash flows while presenting the project in the black and white terms of positive or negative: If the NPV is negative, the project is a non-starter. Likewise, if the NPV is positive, the project creates value for the firm.

The key feature of NPV is that it builds its projected cash flows based on a discount rate or *required rate of return*. Most often the rate of return is the firm's cost of capital. Alternatively, the discount rate might be an accepted hurdle rate. The most commonly used discount rate for NPV analysis is the *weighted average cost-of-capital* (WACC), a blended valuation of the firm's cost of debt, the firm's cost of equity, and the firm's corporate tax advantages.

NOTE	Although an in-depth discussion of capital structure valuation is out of the scope of this book, a brief explanation of cost of capital can help explain the role of the rate of return in NPV analysis.
	The firm's cost of capital is the portion of one dollar of investment by a firm that belongs to the firm's shareholders and creditors. Companies of similar size and in related industries might have a comparable cost of capital; however, each firm's cost of capital is unique and exclusive to that firm.
	WACC is the most commonly used method to measure cost of capital and is the rate of return typically used in NPV analysis. The formula for WACC is as follows:
	Total WACC = (Cost of Equity * Percentage Equity) + (Cost of Debt * Percentage Debt) * (1 – Tax Rate)

After the rate of return is determined, the cash flows are then discounted over the life of the project based on the required rate of return.

NPV is fairly simple despite the intimidating formula. Because NPV is not "napkin math," the preferred method of calculating NPV is to use a spreadsheet or a business calculator. The formula for NPV is:

$$NPV = \sum_{t=0}^{T} \frac{CF_1}{(1 + rate)^1} = CF_0 + \frac{CF_1}{(1 + rate)^1} + \frac{CF_2}{(1 + rate)^2} + \frac{CF_3}{(1 + rate)^3} \ldots \frac{CF_1}{(1 + rate)^1}$$

For example, if a new disk system that cost $5,000 is expected to increase performance for an online transactional system, resulting in cash inflows over $2500 over three years, and the firm's WACC is 12 percent, the NPV is calculated as:

$$NPV = -5000 + \frac{833.33}{(1 + .12)^1} + \frac{833.33}{(1 + .12)^2} + \frac{833.33}{(1 + .12)^3}$$

$$NPV = -\$2496.23$$

The NPV for this project is negative; therefore, the company should not do the project.

Let us perform NPV analysis on the Goodrich Waterfront project for a final example. Year 0 of the project sees a total capital outlay of $1,500,000 and subsequent cash inflows of $1,500,000, $250,000, and $250,000 in years one, two, and three, respectively. The revised cash flows for years two and three are negative, however, after including the outrageous licensing and maintenance charges.

The required rate of return for Goodrich is ten percent. The net present value of the Waterfront project is calculated as follows:

$$NPV = -1,500,000 + \frac{1,500,000}{(1+.10)^1} + \frac{-750,000}{(1+.10)^2} + \frac{-250,000}{(1+.10)^3}$$

NPV = -$1,500,000 + 1,363,636.36 + -619.83471 + -187,828.70

NPV = -$944,027.05

NPV analysis, by taking into account the time value of money and the firm's required rate of return, provides a much more realistic view of the financial impact of the project. Because the NPV is negative, the $1,500,000 invested in Waterfront would actually lose the firm money. The Waterfront project can be seen for what it is: a significant capital outlay that destroys more value than it creates.

NOTE   Note that for IT-related projects, NPV analysis is typically carried out over three years to match the depreciation schedule and the useful life of the assets involved. For larger projects (such as constructing a new building) or for purchases of other assets with lengthy depreciation schedules (such as real estate), longer time horizons are used.

There are a number of reasons NPV is not widely used to measure IT projects. Many people are unfamiliar with NPV or tend to have the misperception that it is hard to use and the required rate of return is not often freely available. The primary reason NPV is not widely used to measure IT projects, however, is that projected cash flows for non-revenue impacting environments are difficult to estimate. Storage networking projects, however, are ideally suited for NPV analysis because of the tangible benefits mentioned earlier: primarily increased utilization, and, if the cost of downtime is measurable, increased availability. These expense reduction and cost avoidance benefits can be treated as cash inflows over the life of the project.

Economic Value Added

EVA is a framework for measuring a company's financial performance. This method is copyrighted by Stern, Stewart, and Company. EVA is a management tool and a financial metric, but at its essence, it is a benchmark for measuring productivity—the creation of value at a firm.

The concepts behind EVA analysis are not new. They have been floating around for some time. Peter Drucker, management guru and supporter of EVA efforts, notes in his essay, "The Information Executives Truly Need," that "...The last generation of classical economists, Alfred Marshall in England and Eugen Böhm-Bawerk in Austria, were already discussing [the principle ideas behind EVA analysis] in the late 1890s."[1]

EVA is a method of valuing a company's *economic* profit versus accounting profits, as recorded in SEC filings. Economic profit is the creation of shareholder value, whereas accounting profits might or might not reflect economic value or profit. Accounting profits are inflated by credit and tax advantages that do not include the firm's cost of capital (and can be manipulated with malicious intent).

Like Six Sigma, which aims to decrease error rates and increase productivity across the whole enterprise, or Total Quality Management (TQM), which has similar aims, EVA analysis does encompass the performance of the whole firm. EVA is not, however, strictly a performance management trend. EVA analysis picks up financial measurement where ROI and NPV leave off by factoring in the cost of purchasing and using capital and by measuring the performance of all projects, products, and divisions of the firm using the same benchmark rate.

Drucker states quite plainly that, "Until a business returns a profit that is greater than its cost of capital, it operates at a loss. Never mind that it pays taxes as if it had a genuine profit. The enterprise still returns less to the economy than it devours in resources."[2]

Because EVA analysis is typically used to measure the value of the firm's output, the formal equation for EVA analysis uses something called NOPAT (net operating profit after taxes):

EVA = Net Operating Profit After Taxes − (Capital * Cost of Capital)

Because the IT department typically does not sell a product or a service on the open market or pay taxes separately from the firm as a whole, you need to modify the EVA equation to apply EVA to internal infrastructure projects.

NOTE	Even a department that uses a chargeback mechanism for its goods and services needs to modify the EVA measurement because an internal department typically does not operate at a profit.

To use EVA to measure the impact of an IT project, the operating profit or net inflows have to be measured in terms of cost avoidances and cost savings. As with NPV analysis, the net benefits from the project, primarily increased utilization, still require a dollar value. The revised calculation looks like this:

Revised EVA = Net Benefits – (Capital * Cost of Capital)

Net benefits are the sum total of all cash inflows, cost avoidances, and cost reductions related to the project. The capital charge in the equation is the obvious capital expenditure associated with the project. New hardware, new software, new datacenter—any costs that cannot be expensed and must be depreciated need to be included here.

For an example, let us apply EVA to the Goodrich cash register example:

EVA = Net Benefits – (Capital * Cost of Capital)

EVA = $4000 – ($2500 * 10.0 percent)

EVA = $3750

The economic profit of investing in the new cash register is actually only $3750, not $4000. Note that the economic profit (the EVA) from investing in the cash register is less than the accounting profit. EVA analysis presents the investment in terms of value added to the shareholders.

Metrics, such as ROI, can be refined to account for EVA.

The ROI for the cash register investment is 60 percent—($4000 – $2500) / $2500. The EVA-adjusted ROI for the cash register project is calculated as follows:

EVA-Adjusted ROI = ($3750 – $2500) / $2500

ROI = 50.00 percent

Let us apply EVA to the Waterfront project. (Note that the cash flows here are treated as one-time events).

The Waterfront project has capital outlays of $1,500,000 and increased revenue streams of $1,500,000 in the first year, and –$750,000 and –$250,000 in each of the two subsequent years:

EVA = Net Benefits – (Capital * Cost of Capital)

EVA = $–1,000,000 – ($1,500,000 * 10.0 percent)

EVA = –$1,150,000

You do not need to calculate the EVA-adjusted ROI: The EVA of the Waterfront project is, as expected, a negative number, which indicates that Goodrich would destroy economic value by investing in Waterfront.

EVA is most beneficial when used across the entire firm. An EVA firm is capable of more accurately measuring the impact of all of its investments on shareholder value. EVA analysis can be used, however, to measure the value of individual projects and, when used together with ROI and NPV, EVA provides another level of accountability for capital investments.

This chapter uses these metrics to build four simple value cases. Selecting the appropriate metric for value case analysis is up to the firm's finance or management teams. The following examples, however, use each of the three metrics appropriate for measuring the impact of large projects (ROI, NPV, EVA). The use of multiple metrics often helps present a stronger case for management.

Value Case Analysis

The following sections demonstrate how to build a value case using ROI, NPV, and EVA for each of the following four types of projects:

- Direct-attached storage (DAS)-to-SAN migration
- Storage consolidation
- DAS-to-Network-attached storage (NAS) migration
- Internet SCSI (iSCSI) implementation

DAS-to-SAN Migration Value Case

The first of these value case examples examines the benefits of migrating from DAS to SAN in the following environment.

The Goodrich firm has five terabytes of direct-attached SCSI storage in its main data center, which is spread across ten hosts and two storage frames with older 36-GB drives configured as RAID-protected storage. This storage is only 50 percent allocated with all ports utilized. One of these hosts serves as a backup media server and drives a tape library. The Goodrich IT department has determined that its per MB TCO for this storage environment (including labor, backup, power, cooling and facilities, and hardware and software maintenance) is $0.10 per MB. The fully burdened annualized cost for the entire environment is $512,000.00.

NOTE	For the sake of easy math, I do not factor in the depreciation for the hardware in these items, although in reality, the TCO reflects the depreciation expense.

The staff realizes that it needs to do something about the poor allocation efficiency and wants to share this storage with another group that needs access to some of the same data sets. The team wants to create a separate development environment for a new application that they are building, which already has spare server capacity but needs additional storage.

The four-member technical team at Goodrich has investigated the idea of putting this storage onto a SAN to help share the data with other groups and increase the overall allocation efficiency of the environment. The team has a limited budget, but believes it can accomplish its goals using two fixed 32-port switches. Only two members of the team, however, are intimately familiar with managing storage on a SAN; the other two members of the team require training that costs $1000 per person.

The incremental cost of the Fibre Channel switches is $64,000 ($1000 per port). The facilities costs are negligible, especially if the environment is already Fibre Channel and there is no requirement for extra cabling. In this case, because the environment is SCSI, Goodrich requires 20 new FC host bus adapters (two on each of the ten hosts) and four new FC adapters for the two disk frames.

The capital costs and expenses for the migration are shown in Table 3-3.

Table 3-3   *Sample Migration Costs*

Item	Cost
Storage	$512,000.00
Switches	$64,000.00
Training	$2000.00
HBAs	$20,000.00
FAs	$20,000.00
Total	$618,000.00
Total Storage (MB)	5,000,000
Per MB TCO	$0.12

The incremental costs of the migration are $106,000. Coupled with the previous fully burdened annualized cost of $512,000, the incremental costs bring the fully burdened TCO for this environment to $618,000, a $0.02 per MB increase (raising the TCO from $0.10 to $0.12).

The technical team, however, realizes that the SAN increases the allocation efficiency significantly and since discovering that their storage is only 50 percent allocated with all available ports in use, they realize they must recalculate the TCO. When factoring in for the allocation efficiency, the current per MB TCO is actually $0.25. Table 3-4 shows the revised Goodrich TCO.

Table 3-4   *Revised Goodrich TCO*

Item	Cost
Storage	$512,000.00
Switches	$64,000.00
Training	$2000.00
HBAs	$20,000.00
FAs	$20,000.00

Table 3-4   *Revised Goodrich TCO (Continued)*

Item	Cost
Total	$618,000.00
Total Storage (MB)	5,000,000
Utilization Factor 50 percent (MB)	2,500,000
Per MB TCO	$0.25

If the team determines that a realistic goal for increased utilization is 75 percent, the addition of the storage network actually reduces the total cost of ownership by $0.09 per MB.

Table 3-5 shows the savings (in TCO terms) that Goodrich can achieve by merely installing a SAN to increase utilization.

Table 3-5   *Goodrich Savings by Installing a SAN to Increase Utilization*

Item	Cost
Storage	$512,000.00
Switches	$64,000.00
Training	$2,000.00
HBAs	$20,000.00
FAs	$20,000.00
Total	$618,000.00
Total Storage (MB)	5,000,000
Utilization Factor 75 percent (MB)	3,750,000
Increased Storage	1,250,000
Reduced TCO	$0.16

NOTE	Keep in mind that HBAs and training are treated as expenses and are therefore not depreciated.

In terms of ROI, the results from this analysis are encouraging. The sum of all returns is the increased storage available for use, which with the increase in utilization from 50 percent to 75 percent, equals 1.25 terabytes. If you value the reclaimed storage at the original $0.12 per MB acquisition cost, you see a respectable 41.51 percent ROI for the installation of the SAN.

ROI = (Sum of all Returns – Sum of all Investments) / (Sum of all Investments)

ROI = ($150,000-$106,000)/$106,000

ROI = 41.51 percent

Increasing allocation efficiency decreases the frequency of storage purchases, increases the storage yield, and decreases the cost of poor quality and the TCO.

Let's take another look at the numbers using NPV. Let's assume that Goodrich still has a required rate of return of 10 percent. The cash flow for Year 0 is –$106,000, and the following year, it is $150,000. The NPV for this project over a one-year horizon is calculated as follows:

NPV = –$106,000 + ($150,000 / 1.1)

NPV = $30,363.64

The NPV for this project is positive, which is another indication that Goodrich should implement the SAN. Even if Goodrich is a little more conservative and decides to stretch the returns out over two years, knowing that they will not be able to efficiently utilize all of the storage from the increased allocation, the NPV for this project is still positive:

NPV = –$106,000 + ($75,000 / 1.1) + ($75,000 / 1.1^2)

NPV = $24,165.29

In fact, even if Goodrich decides to carry the returns out over three years (the average useful life of the products in the environment), the NPV is still positive!

EVA analysis shows us the economic value created by the firm when migrating from DAS to SAN. If you use the same returns for the first year, $150,000, and a cost-of-capital of 10 percent, EVA analysis reveals a similarly positive message:

EVA = $150,000 – ($106,000 * 0.10)

EVA = $139,400

The EVA-adjusted ROI shows the true ROI after including the cost of capital:

EVA-Adjusted ROI = ($139,400 − $106,000) / $106,000

EVA-Adjusted ROI = 31.51 percent

The DAS-to-SAN migration should create value for the firm, and it should be started as soon as possible.

As the project matures, the TCO for the new SAN environment needs to include an adjustment for any other associated costs, such as software purchased to manage the environment or any additional headcount added to support the new hardware. Although it is often overlooked, post-project analysis needs to be completed to understand the true impact of the changes to the environment, to measure the delivery of the service against its service level agreement (SLA), and to update the TCO for the environment.

Intangible benefits are difficult to quantify, but this does not mean they cannot be counted in the financial analysis. Depending on the firm's strategy, intangible benefits, such as increased business continuance capabilities (through the implementation of FCIP or another type of SAN extension), can be numerically weighted to provide some type of quantitative value and to distinguish them from alternative projects, which might not help execute a firm's strategy.

For example, if one of the firm's top strategic goals is to increase data security and availability, a project that includes long-distance replication over SAN extensions as part of a disaster recovery plan should be weighted heavier than a disk migration strategy that does not offer replication. The business stakeholders need to be able to assign a dollar value to their business continuance requirements (in terms of cost avoidance measured in dollars per hour downtime), and then assign the appropriate weight to the projects in the project pool. The projects with the highest weighting and the projects with positive NPV, ROI, and EVA are then selected for funding and execution.

Storage Consolidation Value Case

Consolidation offers tangible benefits that can be achieved in a relatively short period of time. In particular, disk consolidation projects can:

- Decrease annual maintenance bills

- Decrease facility expenses

- Decrease points of management
- Improve operational efficiencies

A few years have passed, and Goodrich now has in production and on its books 80 external storage frames, all of which are configured as DAS and are only 60 percent allocated. These 80 frames (comprised of varying sizes of disk from 9 GB to 36 GB) have been fully depreciated; however, they carry monthly maintenance charges of roughly $6000 per month per frame. Goodrich pays a total of $5,760,000 per year in support for these frames.

In terms of TCO, the annual datacenter utilization cost for 80 storage frames is $1,200,000 (80 * 1.5 tiles * $10,000 per tile). Concurrently, the Goodrich IT team is working with the finance department to determine if they can build another datacenter because they have reached capacity in both datacenters and would like to build a backup datacenter. Original estimates indicate that a new backup datacenter would cost Goodrich roughly $4,000,000.

Goodrich is faced with a prime consolidation opportunity here. With larger and faster disks available on the market and with lower purchase prices for storage, Goodrich, using the highest capacity drives available, has the chance to consolidate from 80 frames down to eight.

The acquisition cost of the eight new frames includes three years of hardware and software maintenance and comes to a total of $3,600,000 million. The sum of all returns is the cost avoidance of the maintenance bill—$5,600,000—plus the cost reduction in utilities—$1,008,000 (72 * 1.5 * $10,000).

The ROI for this project is calculated as follows:

ROI = (Sum of all Returns – Sum of all Investments) / (Sum of all Investments)

ROI = ($6,608,000 – $3,600,000)/$3,600,000.

ROI = 83.56 percent

The NPV for this project is calculated just as the other examples, but takes the returns out over all three years:

NPV = –$3,600,000 + ($6,608,000 / 1.1) + ($6,608,000 / 1.1^2) + ($6,608,000 / 1.1^3)

NPV = $12,833,117.96

EVA analysis shows the value of the returns for the first year of the project after accounting for the cost of capital:

EVA = \$6,608,000 – (\$3,600,000 * 0.10)

EVA = \$6,248,000

The EVA-adjusted ROI for the first year is calculated as follows:

EVA-Adjusted ROI = (\$6,248,000.00 – \$3,600,000.00) / \$3,600,000.00

EVA-Adjusted ROI = 73.56 percent

NOTE   On the surface, it appears that Goodrich is deferring maintenance costs indefinitely, and if they choose to consolidate every three years, this would in fact be true. However, Goodrich is not taking advantage of the system; they are merely taking advantage of the new technologies available and decreasing the overhead associated with storage assets by migrating to best-in-breed technologies.

With the creation of a storage network in tandem with the consolidation, Goodrich has the opportunity to increase utilization and lower TCO. The additional costs of SAN hardware needs to be analyzed, but those costs should be completely offset by the increase in utilization and the decrease in the TCO per MB.

Consolidation at both the hardware and the application layer provides ample opportunities to reduce points of management and gain economies of scale. Consolidation at the application level trickles down to the physical layer and releases compute cycles, application licenses, and labor resources from the upkeep and maintenance of applications.

From a storage perspective, driving consolidation from the ground up is a great way to raise awareness of the issues previously discussed (cost-of-capital and TCO) and is a quick way to gain momentum for application and server consolidation efforts. When the staff starts to feel relief from managing fewer components (fewer components mean fewer hardware replacements and fewer outages) and experiences the other benefits of consolidation, other consolidation efforts become an easy sell.

Consolidation, after SAN migration, is the most important storage strategy a company can have.

DAS-to-NAS Migration Value Case

The Goodrich external web site and intranet currently reside on older, external RAID arrays that are configured as direct-attached storage with no mirroring or failover capability. The data in these environments is business-critical and read frequently, but written to infrequently, thus performance is of little concern. As part of the TCO study, the Goodrich IT department found that the TCO for the external storage frames in this environment was significantly higher than they expected. The two frames in this environment have been fully depreciated. The teams developing applications for the web site want multiple copies of data to test against. After discussing various vendor proposals with the team members, IT management has determined that this environment is a good candidate for migration to a NAS solution.

The acquisition cost for a NAS solution with failover capability that matches the requirements of this environment is $0.10 per MB, or $250,000.00, which includes hardware and software maintenance costs and redundant hardware for failover capability.

The sum of all returns for this migration (exclusive of a weighted value for the added functionality of failover capability) is the total cost avoidance for the maintenance on the two older frames of $144,000 per year (2 * $6000 per month * 12 months) or $432,000 over three years.

NOTE   In addition to the decreased acquisitions costs, the benefits from a DAS-to-NAS migration are primarily intangible and difficult to quantify: the flexibility of shared storage, the ease of use and administration, and the economies of scale, which stem from the use of the IP network.

In this case, the maintenance reduction provides the majority of the net benefits of the project.

The scale of this project is such that the ROI becomes positive in the second year. The ROI can be calculated as follows:

ROI = (Sum of all Returns) − (Sum of all Investments) / (Sum of all Investments)

ROI = ($288,000 − $250,000) / $250,000

ROI = 15.20 percent

In the third year, the ROI becomes significant.

ROI = (Sum of all Returns) − (Sum of all Investments) / (Sum of all Investments)

ROI = ($432,000 − $250,000) / $250,000

ROI = 72.80 percent

The NPV for the DAS-to-NAS migration would be:

NPV = −$250,000 + ($144,000 / 1.1) + ($144,000 / 1.1^2) + ($144,000 / 1.1^3)

NPV = $108,106.69

EVA analysis shows us the true economic value of the project:

EVA = Net Benefits − (Capital * Cost of Capital)

EVA = $432,000 − ($250,000 * .10)

EVA = $407,000

The EVA-adjusted ROI is:

ROI = ($407,000 − $250,000) / $250,000

ROI = 62.80 percent

Network-attached storage is an excellent solution for applications for which availability and cost requirements outweigh the need for high performance. NAS hardware typically has a lower purchase price than higher-tiered solutions, which obviously helps to lower the TCO. Other NAS features also lower the storage TCO. Snapshot technology helps to ease labor costs associated with backups to tape and simplifies the process of providing shared storage to other groups that require access to the same data (as when multiple development environments require separate copies of the same code tree).

With IP networks, as with storage, a fundamental piece of TCO is utilization. Underutilized IP networks have a higher TCO than networks that are optimally utilized. With some planning, excess IP capacity can be successfully allocated for NAS storage requirements. Because NAS solutions do not require a buildup of FC capacity and can utilize resources already in place (network cards on the host; cabling, routers, and switches on the network), they are inherently more cost-efficient.

Migration from DAS to NAS, as application requirements dictate, can increase operational efficiencies and lower the overall storage TCO. Coupled with a consolidation effort, ROI numbers for NAS migrations should approach triple digits.

iSCSI Implementation Value Case

Similar to a NAS storage implementation, an iSCSI solution utilizes pre-existing IP infrastructure (hardware, software management tools, and often networking expertise), with the added benefit of requiring no additional FC host-bus adapters for the hosts or additional Fibre Channel switch infrastructure required for a SAN. For applications with less stringent performance requirements, iSCSI can provide a low-cost, easy-to-use storage solution. With the added benefit of being a routable protocol, iSCSI enables the host and the storage to be located great distances apart.

For hosts requiring increased data throughput, *TCP offload engines* (also known as TCP offload engines [*TOE*] *cards*) can be used to relieve some of the processing burden from the host's CPU and from the primary network interface. Even with the added expense of TOE cards, an iSCSI solution can be significantly less expensive than a FC SAN solution. Although prices for FC HBAs are falling, FC HBAs are generally twice the cost of a TOE card and four to five times more costly than a standard Ethernet card.

NOTE   The performance of iSCSI software drivers has increased over time, which means that TOE cards are often not required for many installations.

Goodrich has an excellent opportunity to utilize iSCSI transport in the following example. Goodrich has a number of Wintel platform hosts dedicated to sharing user home directories in its primary datacenter. This environment uses a terabyte of direct-attached storage, but it has reached its full capacity. In its secondary datacenter, Goodrich has an additional terabyte of storage that is only 25 percent utilized. The acquisition cost for one MB of storage is $0.08.

To provide the additional storage for this environment, Goodrich can do one of the following:

- Spend $175,000 for additional direct-attached storage to be hosted in the primary data center

- Spend $40,000 for two 16-port multiprotocol switches that utilize iSCSI to attach to the remote storage

The Goodrich team decides to invest in an iSCSI solution because they already have an extensive IP network with extra capacity for growth and a staff that is familiar with IP networking.

NOTE	The additional port capacity on the IP network required for iSCSI in this example is a minimal cost that does not diminish the financial impact. It has been excluded from the total cost.

The ROI for this investment can be calculated using the cost avoidance of the $175,000, or, more conservatively, using the value of the 750 GB of storage in the secondary datacenter at $0.08 per MB or $60,000.00 (750,000 * 0.08). The total investment is $40,000 for the multiprotocol switches:

ROI = ($60,000 – $40,000) / $40,000

ROI = 50.00 percent

The NPV for the iSCSI migration is calculated as follows:

NPV = -$40,000 + ($60,000 / 1.1)

NPV = $14,545

EVA analysis shows us the true economic value of reclaiming the additional storage:

EVA = Net Benefits – (Capital * Cost of Capital)

EVA = $60,000 – ($40,000 * .10)

EVA = $56,000

The EVA-adjusted ROI is shown as:

ROI = ($56,000 – $40,000) / $40,000

ROI = 40.00 percent

Conclusion

This chapter covered the basics of using financial metrics to measure the business impact of storage networks. The payback method was introduced to build familiarity with the concepts of financial evaluation. The payback method is generally used only for short-term projects with small budgets. ROI, NPV, and EVA were introduced as tools that are most frequently used for evaluating projects with larger budgets and longer time horizons.

The most critical piece of the DAS-to-SAN migration business case is determining the current storage TCO. Even if this number is just an approximation, it serves as the basis for ROI and NPV analysis. Cash inflows are measured as the value of the increase in storage utilized.

Value cases for consolidation projects are built primarily on cost avoidance figures for maintenance bills and decreases in facilities costs. Consolidation, coupled with SAN migration, further increases the net benefit of migrating to storage networks.

NAS and iSCSI implementations take advantage of pre-existing IP infrastructure to lower the TCO. Migrations from DAS to NAS and from DAS to iSCSI can also significantly help increase allocation utilization.

The next step in executing a storage vision is tactical. After the value case is built and the solution is funded, the challenges involved with implementation follow. Available best practices can help navigate the array of possible pitfalls, but true implementation success requires an understanding of your environment and its application requirements in addition to the less technical facets, such as negotiating, pricing, and staffing your project. Best practices for implementing storage networking strategies are covered in Chapter 4, "How it Should Be Done: Implementation Strategies and Best Practices."

End Notes

[1]Reprinted by permission of *Harvard Business Review*. From "The Information Executives Truly Need," by Peter Drucker, January–February 1995. Reprinted by permission of *Harvard Business Review*, Copyright ® 1995 by the Harvard Business School Publishing Corporation; all rights reserved.

[2]ibid.

CHAPTER 4

HOW IT SHOULD BE DONE: IMPLEMENTATION STRATEGIES AND BEST PRACTICES

The previous chapter outlined in broad strokes the differences between several of the storage networking protocols and products available on the market, and demonstrated how to make the business case for deploying them after the architecture has been selected.

This chapter focuses on the tactical aspects of deploying storage networks including the selection of technologies to match business objectives, the process of engaging and negotiating with vendors, and the creation of an internal support model for ongoing support.

Understanding the financial impact of storage networks is only half of the battle. A successful rollout of storage networking technologies is no different than any other successful project in that it requires concrete objectives, detailed planning, and effective communication before, during, and after the fact.

This chapter covers the following topics in detail:

- Technology adoption

- Storage technology primer

- Choosing the right vendor

- Changing the support model paradigm

- Service-level management

- Execution and functional roles

This chapter also provides an overview of current best practices from evaluation and execution to implementation, production deployment, and maintenance. However, before outlining the tactical processes necessary for a successful storage networking project, it is helpful to take a brief look at technology adoption in general.

Technology Adoption

The evolution of a technology and its subsequent adoption to solve a business problem is typically the result of a number of forces acting in tandem. Generally speaking, the process begins with a problem or product gap significant enough to cause stress in a critical business environment. Software and hardware companies analyze that gap and target it with a new product that creates value by relieving the stress caused by that particular issue. In some instances, the vendor might even anticipate customer needs by providing some additional functionality. Further releases of the product follow the same iterative process (identifying product shortcomings and addressing them). In addition, vendors often implement innovations based on feedback from initial customers.

At the same time that vendors develop a product or a suite of products to address an issue, a network of industry media generates sufficient attention toward the new technology so that individuals not closely affiliated with the business stressors have a cursory grasp of the issue that the solution is designed to address.

As timelines progress, communication disperses through trade shows, industry publications, and word of mouth. Both technical resource personnel and management return from trade shows armed with hard data from early adopters. Together the team gains a sense of how the new technology or products perform. More customers adopt the new technology as the product's lifecycle begins the transition from early adopter to early majority, two of the five categories of adopters outlined by Everett Rogers, Distinguished Professor in the Department of Communication and Journalism at the University of New Mexico. In his book, *The Diffusion of Innovation*, Rogers outlines the adoption of innovative ideas by breaking down adopters into the following categories: innovators, early adopters, early majority, late majority, and laggards.[1]

The adoption of technology products and most product lifecycles closely follow Rogers' bell curve, as outlined in Figure 4-1.

Figure 4-1   *Adoption of Innovation*[2]

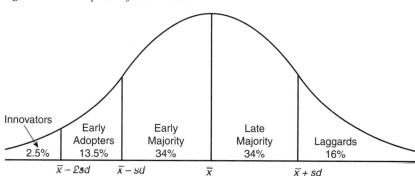

In his monumental book, *Crossing the Chasm*, Geoffrey A. Moore, managing director with The Chasm Group, demonstrates the correlation between the diffusion of innovative ideas and customer segmentation in what is now known as the *Technology adoption lifecycle*.[3]

In this model, early adopters have a combination of needs, curiosity, and resources available to them that motivate and enable them to be on the bleeding edge of a new technology. Early and late majority adopters of products have the benefit of those who have gone before them and can share their knowledge base without suffering the actual pain and expense of product and project failure themselves. Early adopters tend to know what they are getting into when they deploy new products at this stage. Early majority adopters tend to know what they are avoiding—they are generally late to the game on purpose.

In Moore's model, between early adopters and the early majority is the chasm. There is room for disaster on both sides of the chasm; in the event that a product fails to meet expectations, the vendor and the customer both suffer. Products on the market might not be completely hardened or might otherwise be released prematurely. When consumers expect one thing and vendors provide another, a product can suffer irreparable damage to its reputation, customers can lose significant sums of money, and vendors can permanently lose customers.

The ability to choose the right technical solution to effectively solve a business problem is the culmination of many hours of technical and business analysis, as well as years of real-world experience, and a complete understanding of the firm's business environment. Although consultants are useful resources who can be used to implement solutions to solve business problems, in terms of ongoing support, their lack of corporate knowledge might prevent them from solving the problem in the most effective manner possible. The decision-maker for the firm or environment in question should be completely prepared to make decisions regarding the technology, plans for supporting that technology after it has been installed, and the financial impact of installing that technology.

In the long run, as successful products mature and the diffusion of both innovation and business impact information occurs, the adoption rates of new products increase. At this point the chasm is crossed and customers and products move into the majority phase of adoption. It is critical to note that Fibre Channel storage networking products are in the early majority phase of adoption, whereas IP storage networking products are still in the early adopter phase.

As the material in the case studies in Part II shows, many firms can be early adopters of one category of technology and laggards in another category, depending on the criticality of the business need and the ability of certain products and technologies to meet that need.

Chapter 2, "The Business Impact of Storage Networking Technology," discusses the appropriateness of storage networking technologies to solve critical business problems. The following section outlines industry best practices for implementing storage networking technologies.

Storage Technology Primer

This section recaps the various storage technologies previously touched on and places them in a matrix before moving on to the actual implementation discussion.

At the disk level, there are four connectivity options:

- Direct-attached storage (DAS) configured in a one-to-one relationship with the host

- Network-attached storage (NAS) residing on an IP-based network

- Storage Area Network (SAN)-attached storage shared between hosts via a private Fibre Channel network

- SAN-attached storage shared between hosts over a routable IP network

As noted earlier, in addition to being expensive, inefficient, and difficult to scale, DAS presents multiple single points of failure. NAS allows storage to be accessed remotely and utilizes capacity on the IP network infrastructure. Fibre Channel (FC) SANs allow sharing of storage resources over a private Fibre Channel network, increasing allocation efficiency. IP SANs allow for low-cost networked storage as well as the extension of SANs over long distances. Consequently, both FC and IP SANs offer significant advantages over DAS and NAS.

A Fibre Channel SAN infrastructure can be comprised of small independent SAN islands built on fixed Fibre Channel switches (16- and 32-port switches). A SAN infrastructure can also be built by joining multiple larger switches together over interswitch links (ISLs), which are dedicated ports on modular or director-class switches that link switches together. SANs can be extended over long distances via dark fiber or an optical technology, such as Coarse Wave Division Multiplexing (CWDM), Dense Wave Division Multiplexing (DWDM), or Synchronous Optical Network (SONET)/Synchronous Digital Hierarchy (SDH). SANs can also be extended via IP networks using Fibre Channel over IP (FCIP), Internet Fibre Channel Protocol (IFCP), or Internet Small Computer Systems Interface (iSCSI).

IFCP requires a separate gateway device to encapsulate FC frames into IP packets, whereas FCIP typically requires a blade in an existing switch, such as the Cisco MDS 9000 series multiservice switch, to tunnel FC frames via IP. Similarly, iSCSI can either be utilized over a separate device or over a blade in a multiservice switch. All three technologies increase returns to scale by utilizing existing IP capacity and expertise.

NOTE   The term returns to scale is related to economies of scale. It is most commonly used to describe two scenarios. The first scenario is increasing returns to scale whereby the economic output or gain is larger than the labor or capital supplied as input. The second scenario is decreasing returns to scale whereby the economic output is smaller than the labor or capital supplied as input. This scenario is also referred to as *diminishing returns* and is less than desirable.

At the application level, there is storage resource management (SRM) software, SAN management and device management software, and virtualization software. The current manifestation of SRM is perhaps the clearest indication that, at this time, storage software products and consumers are in the chasm—the transition period between early adopter and early majority. SRM software will, as the products mature, provide accurate and up-to-date data on usage trends and allocation and utilization efficiencies. This should greatly ease the pain of capacity planning and provisioning. Although SRM product suites have made great strides, vendors still have a long way to go in addressing customer concerns with their software releases.

SAN management and device management software includes products such as VERITAS SANPoint Control, Tivoli SAN Manager, and Cisco Fabric Manager Server. Products in this category offer performance monitoring and management functionality as well as zoning and provisioning capabilities. In some instances, there might be overlap between the functionality offered by SRM software and that offered by SAN management and device management software.

Storage virtualization software, which is discussed in greater detail in Chapter 5, "Maximizing Storage Investments," simplifies the management of storage devices by abstracting the devices themselves to increase operational efficiencies. Virtualization also reduces capital expenditures by increasing utilization rates. Software products in this category include MonoSphere Storage Manager, VERITAS Storage Foundation for Networks, and IBM SAN Volume Controller.

Table 4-1 highlights the solution types and their application in the enterprise.

Table 4-1   *Storage Solutions Matrix*

Business Need	Solution Format	Solution Technology	Solution Type
Data storage	Hardware	DAS	Expensive disk
Shared data storage	Hardware	FC SANs	Small Fabric, fixed Fibre Channel switch
Shared data storage	Hardware	FC SANs	Large Fabric, modular Fibre Channel switch
Shared, low-cost data storage	Hardware	NAS	Inexpensive, redundant, shared disk
Shared, low-cost data storage	Hardware, Protocol	iSCSI storage network	Small fixed device, blade, multiprotocol modular switch
SAN Extension	Hardware, Protocol	CWDM, DWDM, SONET/SDH, and dark fiber	Optical, long-distance carry
SAN Extension	Hardware, Protocol	iSCSI storage network	Blade, multiprotocol modular switch between hosts, SCSI storage

continues

Table 4-1   *Storage Solutions Matrix*

SAN Extension	Hardware, Protocol	FCIP storage network	Blade, multiprotocol modular switch between Fibre Channel devices
SAN Extension	Hardware, Protocol	IFCP storage network	Gateway device between Fibre Channel devices
SRM	Software	Resource and asset management	Agent devices on hosts
SAN Management	Software	Device management	Centralized device administration and management
Virtualization	Software	Virtualization of resources	Abstraction of resources to increase utilization

Given the array of storage networking solutions on the market designed to solve the inadequacies of DAS, it is critical that one use a business case methodology to evaluate the financial impact of each solution and the appropriateness of the solution to fit the business need. Consequently, the application of storage networking technology must be framed within the discussion of the total cost of ownership (TCO) of the solution. In other words, the costs associated with the solution must match the business need accordingly; the most appropriate way of doing so is with a tiered storage strategy.

TCO, Tiered Storage, and Capacity Planning

Calculating TCO is covered in Chapter 2; however, it is important to take that discussion to the next level. Discussions of TCO eventually lead to the discussion of a tiered storage architecture as part of an Information Lifecycle Management (ILM) framework. In an ILM framework, processes and procedures dictate the movement of information through storage tiers as its criticality and frequency of access decrease over time.

The U.S. Securities Exchange Commission (SEC) regulations and new requirements for compliance with the Sarbanes-Oxley Act and the Health Insurance Portability and Accountability Act (HIPAA) have lengthened retention times for many types of data up to seven years or more. It is not cost effective to store all types of data on the same format for such long periods of time because the criticality of information typically decreases over time. This is not to say that the information becomes worthless as it ages (if a certain record is required after a long period of time, the crucial nature of that information increases tenfold), but the frequency of its access decreases and therefore the nature of the storage solution should change as well. This is a simple cost-benefit analysis. Even much of the information that is considered mission-critical changes little after it is written, and might be accessed infrequently if at all. Abstraction or virtualization of the storage through software can allow an application to transparently access the information even after it is moved to a different tier.

Information Lifecycle Management

ILM is not a new concept; processes similar to those now being introduced as part of an ILM framework have been used by business for years to manage the storage of information. As requirements for retention change and the frequency of access declines, the information moves through a tiered infrastructure. In this manner, the TCO is reduced as hardware solutions at each tier have different cost structures. Ultimately, the information is archived to tape for long-term, offline storage, converted to some type of flat file format for access by any application, or deleted entirely as appropriate. Figure 4-2 outlines a generic tiered, ILM infrastructure.

Figure 4-2   *Tiered Storage and Information Lifecycle Management*

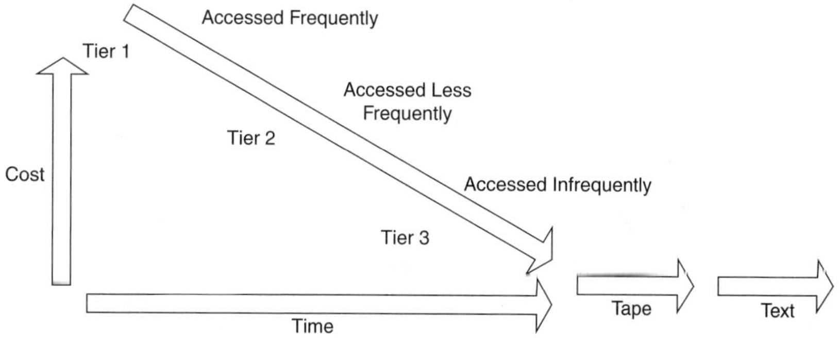

A typical Tier 1 storage platform can be built with highly available, redundant disks, whereas a Tier 2 platform might be the same disks configured in a non-redundant fashion. Tier 3 might be configured with redundant, inexpensive disks such as Serial Advanced Technology Attachment (SATA) drives for online storage of rarely accessed information.

An accompanying strategy for long-term, nearline storage is to modify the data from its original format to release the data from its application-specific requirements. Under this procedure, the contents of the original data records would be scraped into a different file format, such as hypertext markup language (HTML), extensible markup language (XML), or plain text. In the long term, as backup applications expire or are decommissioned, the means to access the data from tape might no longer be available. Converting the contents of the file to a standardized format (without dependence on a vendor-specific solution) enables the data to be more easily retrieved when needed.

Just as there are hardware savings with the tiered storage strategy, there are also returns to scale with regard to management of the data as it moves through each phase of its lifecycle. The management requirements for high performance storage and frequently accessed or briskly growing data far outstrip the associated management requirements of offline (tape storage) technologies. Enterprise Resource Planning (ERP) installations and On-Line Transactional Processing (OLTP) environments require rigorous capacity planning and monitoring, whereas records retained just for the purpose of regulatory compliance require little or no hands-on attention.

Software tools designed to move information through its lifecycle (until the data is finally deleted at the end of its useful life) are slowly coming to market. Independent Software Vendors (ISVs) and Original Equipment Manufacturers (OEMs) are working to build lifecycle management functionality into their current frameworks for storage management. Such software products decrease the management overhead associated with moving data between tiers, and consequently lower the TCO throughout the entire lifecycle.

As mentioned previously, the final stage of the information lifecycle is to delete the record or file and reclaim the associated storage. Deletion of the file when the requirements for retention have expired is mandatory to release the costs associated with this storage and to relieve the burden on the storage management team.

An essential component of planning for a storage networking project, after addressing the need for a tiered infrastructure, is planning for performance.

Performance Planning

Critical to supporting a tiered infrastructure and managing information through its lifecycle is the ability to accurately size an application based on its performance traits (such as heavy writes in online transaction processing, a lot of reads in data warehousing, or bursts of reads and writes in batch processing). In addition, it is necessary to match the storage subsystem to the functional requirements of the application (high availability, near line, length of retention).

Estimating an application's performance requirements can be done simply by running systems tools such as, system activity reporter (SAR), to find IO rates over a set period of time, then sizing appropriately to handle periods of peak throughput based on the block size of the application. Similarly, the same type of data can be collected at the database level with regard to cache hits and misses.

Alternately, capacity planning and application sizing can be done with proprietary capacity planning tools or by using capacity planning frameworks, such as those offered by Teamquest or BMC Software. Depending on the nature of the environment, if one of these larger frameworks is not already installed, it is highly unlikely that it is worth buying and installing one just to size a solution prior to investing in a SAN. Ultimately, upon maturity, SRM software and SAN management software greatly simplify the process of capacity planning for SAN environments.

Using system tools and doing the math required to accurately size and plan for disk and IO throughput prior to installing a SAN are relatively straightforward processes. The final requirement for performance planning is a holistic understanding of the application environment, which is where corporate knowledge plays a big role. When are the backup windows? When are the periods of peak processing? When was the last time the system was upgraded? This type of data is crucial to solid analysis and cannot be completely obtained through the use of software. Although this information might not be inherently quantifiable, it can help increase the granularity of your quantitative analysis and help make a better business decision.

Oversubscription

Another aspect of performance planning is oversubscription. Over-subscription in the SAN arena, just as in LAN or WAN networking, is a capacity planning technique that guarantees a minimum rate of throughput to an application or set of applications, while at the same time provisioning for an estimated maximum rate of throughput. In other words, the capacity of the network is oversold under the assumption that not all applications burst and reach maximum throughput at the same time. In this way, provisions are made for maximum bandwidth demand with significantly less infrastructure cost.

The following is a generic example designed to illustrate the concept of oversubscription exclusive of the concept of Quality of Service (QOS). Also note that oversubscription, in the context of host to switch connectivity, is often referred to as the *fan-in* or *fan-out ratio*.

A small SAN-island backbone (64 2-Gbps ports on a director-class switch) is oversubscribed to five applications on each of six hosts. Each application's demand bursts at 2 Gbps on each channel for a total application demand of 60 Gbps (6 hosts × 5 applications × 2 Gbps), as shown in Figure 4-3.

Figure 4-3 *Oversubscription*

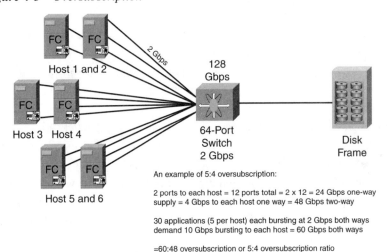

An example of 5:4 oversubscription:

2 ports to each host = 12 ports total = 2 x 12 = 24 Gbps one-way
supply = 4 Gbps to each host one way = 48 Gbps two-way

30 applications (5 per host) each bursting at 2 Gbps both ways
demand 10 Gbps bursting to each host = 60 Gbps both ways

=60:48 oversubscription or 5:4 oversubscription ratio

The aggregate bandwidth supplied over two connections to each host is 48 Gbps full duplex (2 ports × 2 Gbps × 6 hosts = 24 Gbps half duplex). Therefore, with the configuration shown in Figure 4-3, you have a 5:4 oversubscription ratio.

By providing a minimum committed information rate you are also providing for a maximum information rate based on assumptions about characteristic application performance. Figure 4-3 demonstrates this concept.

NOTE   In the real world, special operating system tools and application scheduling software is required to manage application level planning for oversubscription. Mapping application requirements to bandwidth restrictions is currently beyond the scope of SAN software and hardware.

The concept of oversubscription also applies when dealing with ISLs. ISLs, as mentioned earlier, are interswitch links or ports on a switch reserved for connections to other switches, and are used for building large fabrics. If the small SAN island in our previous example is expected to scale to two 64-port directors, then a minimum of two ports on each switch (four ports total) are required to link the switches together for half-duplex bandwidth of 4 Gbps. Depending on the amount of maximum overall throughput required now and in the future, it might be necessary to reserve as many as 16 ports for ISLs for greater bandwidth. Figure 4-4 demonstrates the use of ISLs to provide connectivity and throughput for a larger fabric.

Figure 4-4   *Oversubscription with ISLs*

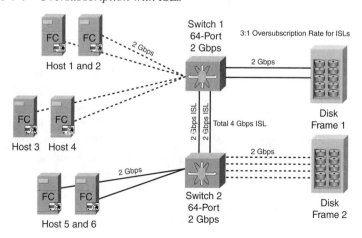

In this diagram, two director-class switches are linked together with ISLs to provide connectivity to the two disk cabinets on the right. Hosts 1 through 4 are attached through Switch 1 at the top to both Disk Frame 1 and Disk Frame 2 via the ISLs between Switch 1 and Switch 2. Hosts 5 and 6 are attached to both Disk Frame 1 and Disk Frame 2 via the ISL between Switch 1 and Switch 2. There is a committed information rate of 4 Gbps half-duplex over the ISLs.

If the applications in this environment all burst at the same time there is a bandwidth demand of 12 Gbps while the ISLs can only provide 4 Gbps. In this particular instance, it is important to note that the 4 Gbps ISL bandwidth is a possible bottleneck for all hosts using the ISLs.

If the application environments and storage subsystems are appropriately sized then oversubscription provides the proper bandwidth at the least cost. If not, and if the traffic between the hosts and the disk frames is sustained at greater than 4 Gbps (possibly during a backup window) then there will be congestion on the ISL link.

If significant throughput is required, this environment is undersized and requires a different architecture. The entire backbone could be replaced with an intelligent switch platform, a director-class switch with 140 ports such as the McData Intrepid 6140, or the Cisco MDS 9509, which is configurable with up to 224 ports.

Bear in mind that increasing the number of ISLs raises the average per port cost of the solution insofar as ISLs are ports consumed solely for interswitch communication and cannot be doled out directly to the host or the storage device.

In summary, oversubscription is one way of cost-effectively allocating bandwidth supply to environments without purchasing dedicated resources to meet anticipated maximum demand. In this manner it is possible to keep the TCO to a minimum and still supply a maximum information rate at times of peak load.

NOTE	Oversubscription is a term often used in a pejorative sense, but it should be emphasized that oversubscription is not inherently evil. Oversubscription does cause problems when an environment is oversubscribed to the point of causing congestion, and changes in an application that cause unpredicted periods of peak processing can disrupt the model service levels built into an oversubscribed architecture. There is nothing inherently wrong with oversubscription, however; it is an industry best practice commonly used to contain costs.

Depending on the application environment, the amount of throughput required, and the amount of oversubscription needed to avoid congestion, either a core topology or a core-edge topology (the two most common SAN topologies) can be implemented. A brief overview of each topology follows before a discussion of the differences between redundancy and resiliency.

Core Topology

The previous examples demonstrated a core topology using a single FC switch at the core of the architecture. Core topology SANs may also use a large SAN fabric built on multiple core switches linked together by ISLs. Both of these scenarios are demonstrated in Figure 4-5.

Figure 4-5   *Core Topology*

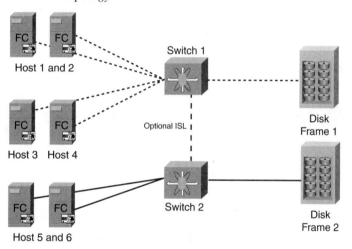

NOTE	It is important to note that these examples require additional switches for redundancy and separate fabrics for resiliency.

The primary advantage of a core topology is fewer points of management. This architecture works well in an environment with a fewer number of hosts accessing large amounts of data. With a core topology, the process of designing and provisioning for application performance for a small number of hosts, allocating ISLs, and managing oversubscription is significantly easier than in a core-edge topology.

One significant disadvantage to a core topology is the cost of expansion as capacity needs increase. Adding additional core switches can be expensive, and reallocating ports across the environment can be labor-intensive.

Core-Edge Topology

A core-edge topology, as shown in Figure 4-6, works well in an environment with a large number of hosts accessing small amounts of data. To provide adequate service to all hosts, as well as face the challenge of locality and many fiber runs across the datacenter back to the core, smaller departmental, fixed, or edge switches are inserted at fixed points in the topology to provide fan-in to many hosts.

Figure 4-6 *Core-Edge Topology*

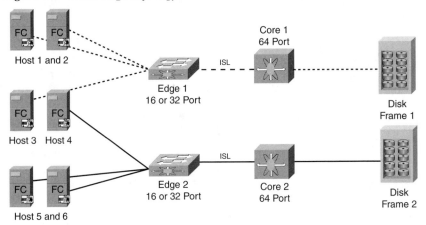

As you can imagine, the process of calculating application throughput over multiple edge switches going back to a single core (or a core comprised of a few director-class switches) becomes challenging quite quickly as more hosts are attached to the SAN. ISL throughput becomes crucial as the number of hosts increases.

The advantage of a core-edge topology should be obvious: with many hosts that have less stringent performance requirements, it is possible to build a cost-effective storage network by adding smaller fixed FC switches as capacity requirements dictate. The disadvantage to this topology should also be obvious: the overhead involved with increased points of management is not trivial. The additional cost of increased ISL throughput is also significant.

In the example in Figure 4-6, ISL allocation becomes quite costly, adding to the TCO of this environment. For example, if the required ISL throughput reaches 8 Gbps, then four ISLs would be required at the edge. If the per port cost is $1000, then the TCO for this environment increases by $4000, as these ports cannot be allocated to the hosts using storage, but can be used only for switch-to-switch communication.

Other topologies include mesh, star, bus (chain) and collapsed-core. Whereas mesh, star and bus topologies are rarely used, the collapsed-core is used more often. The collapsed-core is essentially a combination of core and core-edge topologies with an intelligent switch platform at the core and a suitable mix of 16- and 32-port line cards in the same chassis.

Redundancy and Resiliency

In the discussion of topologies, it is important to understand the nature of redundancy and resiliency in building a SAN architecture as well as the cost differences between these two features.

Previous examples glossed over the topic of redundancy to simplify the concepts of core and core-edge topologies. In these examples, redundant hardware is needed to provide for maximum availability and uptime, while a resilient architecture protects against a single component failure.

To implement full redundancy, there must be at least one additional switch with separate power, separate networking, and multiple paths from the hosts as shown in Figure 4-7. This design also utilizes a separate fabric at each core that prevents failures associated with single-fabric service outages. Multipathing software such as VERITAS DMP or EMC PowerPath provides for multiple paths to the disk at the operating system level, which provides path failover capability at the host level. Obviously, with redundant hardware at each level from the host bus adapter (HBA) to the disk, this solution has the highest price tag. But this solution also provides the best protection against failure and interruption in service, and is a suitable architecture for a Tier 1 infrastructure requiring maximum availability.

Figure 4-7 *Redundant Architecture*

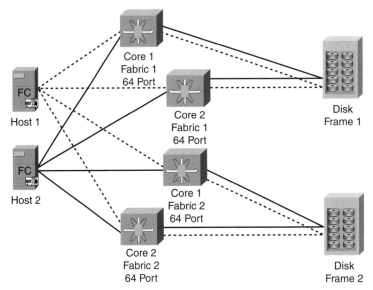

A resilient architecture, on the other hand, provides for recovery from failure in either path without providing full redundancy at the fabric level. As shown in Figure 4-8, the two core switches are joined together into a single fabric that provides fault recovery, but not full failover capabilities. In this example, a resilient architecture is capable of protecting against a single software or hardware failure.

A fully redundant architecture provides maximum protection for the entire solution but at a significantly higher cost than a resilient architecture. The high TCO for such an environment must match the business requirements; otherwise, a less costly solution should be architected. Depending on the revenue associated with a particular environment and the service level agreement (SLA) guiding the delivery of the services residing on the SAN architecture in question, the business needs to perform a cost-benefit analysis and potentially make a choice between the two types of architectures.

Figure 4-8   *Resilient Architecture*

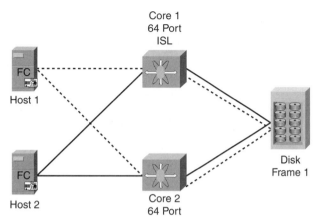

As both solutions need to scale to provide added throughput and additional storage for growth, the cost advantages of resiliency (and the cost disadvantages of redundancy) become apparent. Still, for maximum availability, a redundant solution is the best choice. Depending on the business requirements, however, there might not be an opportunity to choose between the two. A highly available ERP environment requires a highly available SAN and likely requires a redundant architecture. A development environment with fewer performance and availability restrictions might find a resilient architecture sufficient in terms of recoverability and scalability.

Thus far this chapter covered in detail the concepts behind ILM, as well as the most commonly used topologies and architectures. In highlighting the advantages and disadvantages of each solution, you are now prepared to make an informed decision regarding implementation steps, the first of which is choosing the right vendor.

Choosing the Right Vendor

With these basic concepts of SAN architecture and design, a cursory understanding of your own application's requirements and your environment's TCO (or TCO target), it is time to begin the "request-for-x" process and the search for the right product-vendor match. The most commonly completed steps in this process are as follows:

1 Request for Information

2 Request for Proposal

3 Request for Quote

It is best to begin the "request-for-x" process with a proper understanding of your own environment. As vendors become engaged with your project, they are likely to ask many of the same questions touched upon here.

Request for Information (RFI)

The request for information (RFI) should be fully scoped to target a specific application or group of applications, and provide an appropriate matrix for weighting the importance of each application's requirements. For example, an application requiring maximum uptime with no concern for performance would weight availability higher than performance.

An RFI should also provide some historical background regarding the application environments such as long-term trending analysis, any changes in the application client base, and the stated reason for the architectural change. If the goal of the project is to maximize ROI and minimize TCO, you should provide additional information and consult with the vendor's professional services teams about the benefits of consolidation and other storage strategies designed to lower TCO. Do not be afraid to go into detail about the nature of the requirements; thorough communication through every phase of the request process benefits the requestor in the long run.

The pre-sales technical team supporting the vendors you engage will want to know as many specifics as possible before making a recommendation, and therefore should have contact with senior-level technical resources throughout the information gathering phase of the project. After the initial meeting, you should source the information flow through a primary or central contact rather than have the vendor's sales and technical team constantly peppering the members of your technical staff with questions. A project manager or senior technical architect is a good candidate to collect and manage the information flow during the RFI phase.

It might also be beneficial to have technical representation from the clients, so that when a final platform is selected, all stakeholders have ample time to add appropriate input.

NOTE	A vendor management office, if your company has one, might be another good candidate for ownership of the collection of information during the RFI phase.

It is also critical during this stage to evaluate a vendor's certification policy for third-party products. Doing so can likely prevent serious delays during the actual implementation phase.

Finally, the RFI should have a clearly stated start date and end date. Vendors who miss the deadline for submitting the RFI are prevented from participating in the next stage, the Request for Proposal/Request for Quote (RFP/RFQ) process.

RFP/RFQ

If a single vendor meets the criteria based on the RFI process, you can go directly to the RFQ stage. Assuming multiple vendors have been selected based on the criteria outlined in the RFI, an RFP (and eventually an RFQ) should be sent to the vendors making the initial cut.

The RFP/RFQ should also be accurately scoped and should provide realistic timelines and budgetary constraints. You should set forth as soon as possible, whether you are seeking professional services in addition to hardware or if your team does the implementation. It is also critical to spell out the basis of selection in detail to level the playing ground. If the criteria are price and performance, then the vendor whose product has the highest performance and the lowest price should win the purchase order. A granular weighting scale eases the decision-making process.

In addition to application requirements, it is critical to select a vendor on the basis of the product's adherence to industry standards. Adherence to industry standards increases the product's end-to-end manageability and increases operational efficiency.

To increase operational efficiency, or at least not negatively impact current efficiency rates, a storage networking solution should seamlessly fit into your environment's management framework, in addition to providing its own management interface.

It is also customary during this time to create a test bed with sample data from the environment and allow the vendors to present a solution onsite for measurement and quantification of actual performance of the system. Even a scaled down version of an actual environment with data sets comparable to those used in production can give an adequate overview of a system's performance potential. It is critical that the vendors know what tools are used to measure performance and that the same tools be used on each test bed for each vendor. You need to document and clearly communicate the tools and processes used for measurement.

TIP   Keep in mind that the "bakeoff phase" is typically the most interesting phase of this process and, not surprisingly, technical resource teams find it the most enjoyable. As such it should also have a clearly defined start and end date. What is to be measured as well as the tools to be used for measurement must be commonly agreed upon well in advance of this phase of the project to avoid "analysis paralysis."

Finally, it is essential that the team doing the selection adhere to the original constraints of the RFI and RFP. It is neither professional nor beneficial to the success of the project to change the criteria of selection midway through the selection process. It should be clear that after the decision is made, there will be no opportunity for counter bids.

NOTE   Again, a vendor management organization might be more adept at pricing and negotiation and, if so, might free up critical cycles from the technical leadership team.

Changing the Support Model Paradigm

As part of the process of moving from early adopter to early majority, storage networking consumers have much to consider during migration and implementation. In addition to varying degrees of standards in hardware Management Information Bases (MIBs) and software drivers, as well as varying degrees of maturity in management software, one of the most crucial issues is support—the care and feeding of the storage networking solution after product selection and implementation.

Networking and IP Transport Model

Most companies already have some sort of networking or transport support model in place. As more and more storage networks require a long-range networking component (storage over IP or SONET/SDH), storage networking support might fall to the networking infrastructure team. There are some benefits to be reaped from this model. Online support structures and case queues might already be in place. In addition, IP networking knowledge and expertise can be utilized thereby increasing the quality of support. Economies of scale and scope can be achieved with this model, which can boost productivity in the long run.

The issue with this support model, however, is that the end products of networking and of storage are different. The product of the IP network is the IP network—the delivery of IP bandwidth at a set level of service. The end product of the storage network is, of course, storage. Its delivery to the host and application is highly integrated at both the physical and the application layers.

This is not to say that networking support staff cannot be trained or the support structure modified to support applications above the switching layer, but more than likely, that investment is difficult to justify. The level of changes necessary to make joint storage and networking support teams work would likely diminish the capabilities of the current infrastructure support teams while being cost- and time-prohibitive.

This commingling of resources would be advantageous only in small-to medium-sized businesses where the number of IT support staff is limited. For larger environments, alternative support models should be considered.

Virtual Storage Team

Many organizations find the provisioning and performance tuning needs of storage-intensive applications and environments to be met satisfactorily by the system owners—the systems administrators themselves. These individuals already have an intimate knowledge of the applications and the hosts, a wide body of corporate knowledge, a sense of ownership over the system, and, often, the ability to tune performance on-the-fly. Generally speaking, the system owners know the application stakeholders and the end users and have a long history providing quality service to all parties involved.

At a certain level, a systems administration team working only part-time on storage, or a virtual storage team, can meet or exceed expectations as far as ongoing storage support is concerned.

There are three caveats with this support model, however. The first of these is the risk of stovepiping. When the storage support model is a virtual team or comprised only of system owners, there are roadblocks to sharing knowledge, best practices, and expertise. Standards become hard to follow and systems tend to be managed differently, preventing any return to economies of scale. Individuals find it hard to manage systems that are not their own, and they therefore tend to get possessive over their own systems.

The second caveat to take into consideration here is the risk of inefficient storage management. In a virtual support model, storage is often not viewed as a capital asset, and as such, it is not uncommon to find a number of gigabytes stashed away to be doled out to applications at the last second. The hoarding of storage prevents any kind of meaningful capacity planning from taking place, and it drives up the TCO for the environment. It can increase the allocation efficiency in the short run, but in the long run it makes the costs of storage and storage support unmanageable.

The third and final caveat to be aware of with a virtual team is that a virtual team by nature is resource-constrained. Because resources are not fully dedicated to storage management, progress toward a storage vision will likely be impaired by the use of part-time resources.

Depending on the size of your storage environment, a virtual team of storage administrators might work well for your organization. As your firm's storage inventory approaches 500 TB to 1 PB, however, the ability to provide adequate storage support and service diminishes. It is at this point that storage support becomes a full-time job. Decision makers managing environments in excess of 500 TB should investigate creating a full-time storage support team.

Dedicated Storage Team

The concept of a storage team is popular in the distributed computing environment, and it was borrowed from the mainframe world in which it was often customary to have a team of storage-focused individuals dedicated to providing data storage expertise, capacity planning, and support to mission-critical applications. Until recently, many client-server environments had not reached a point where data storage needs overwhelmed a dedicated systems administration team. However, as shown in Chapter 1, "Industry Landscape: Storage Costs and Consumption," the rampant growth of data storage across all industries highlights the fact that many environments are now faced with the inability to adequately support and manage the storage filling the environment.

A dedicated storage support team has the benefit of common or shared knowledge and expertise, as well as a clear charter and a mission statement. It is critical for the success of a dedicated storage team to have executive sponsorship as well as a central repository of tools and experiential data designed to preserve and document repeatable tasks and build a basis for sharing best practices.

Ultimately, a dedicated storage team should be able to drive overall productivity in the environment. Projects or programs, such as storage recovery and storage consolidation, are extremely difficult to support without a dedicated storage support team.

Individuals assigned to a full-time storage team should be able to bring increasing returns to scale to the enterprise hosting arena as the amount of terabytes managed by one individual increases. Ultimately, a dedicated storage support team is able to manage far more terabytes than a virtual team or a systems administration team supporting storage on a part–time basis.

From an organizational standpoint, the creation of a storage support team can face some challenges because the systems administrators might feel that his role is diminished and that the environment is becoming a "black box."

This is a real issue. In the client-server environment, systems administrators can resent storage administrators doing their job. They can also present non-trivial hurdles for storage administrators in terms of both non-assistance as well as impedance (physically denying access to the host or politically undermining attempts to do the work).

Nonetheless, as enterprise storage environments increase in size, a dedicated storage team is likely to provide the best support. Outsourced personnel can augment a dedicated team as well, as need dictates.

Outsourced Professional Services

The storage service provider (SSP) market, which originally seemed promising from an investor's standpoint, quickly soured as customers and then venture capital both evacuated the market almost overnight. The entire service provider market seemed to fall victim of the chasm.

Although the SSP business model offered mission-critical storage services to smaller companies lacking capital resources, such as datacenters and large external storage frames, three issues prevented that model from taking flight in any serious capacity, as follows:

- The first issue was that many companies felt uncomfortable storing mission-critical data, especially intellectual property, financial data, and other sensitive information outside of their own premises.

- The second issue facing SSPs was that they often could not realize the break-even point with a pay-per-use model because firms with significant data storage requirements generally already owned their own storage and datacenters and vice-versa (those who did not have massive amounts of critical data did not need mission-critical datacenter storage).

- The final issue with this model (and probably the most telling) was that, generally, the customers who signed up for SSP services were dot-coms with insignificant revenue streams incapable of supporting the SSPs who incurred severe expenses building excess capacity that was never sold.

From a storage support standpoint, customers today can choose to leverage a partially or fully outsourced model on the premises, or utilize the SSP for complete handoff, or engage a combination of the two solutions.

Outsourcing or outtasking (outsourcing only specific tasks) to a vendor can increase returns to scale, especially if the vendor's services are included as part of a larger contract and can be acquired at little or no extra cost. Outtasking specifically can increase returns to scale because the internal staff resources already assigned to projects can be released and reassigned to critical initiatives requiring more internal expertise (which also allows internal staff to grow, broadening their skill sets and increasing job satisfaction).

Migrating to a completely outsourced or SSP model can lead to some of the same support and control issues seen with the hand-off from system administrators to a dedicated storage team, primarily that the storage environment becomes a black box to the internal support staff. Typically, this solution is used only in a scenario where the firm is in a change-intensive transition period with bursts of growth that cannot be accurately modeled for forecasting purposes. Alternately, an outsourced model might succeed during a period of contraction, when declining revenues are likely to hamper the ability to provide best-in-breed support to applications and end users.

NOTE   The support model for storage networks is different in almost every company. Many companies have so little storage or are so early in the migration and implementation phases that they have not needed to choose a support model.

Data storage at Cisco saw triple-digit growth in 2001 and 2002. Accordingly, the team moved from a virtual storage support team to a fully dedicated storage support team in late 2001. In addition, it increasingly used an outtasked model to offload meticulous and mundane or less strategic labor-intensive tasks. The Cisco storage support model and some of the successes achieved by using that model are discussed in Chapter 8, "Cisco Systems, Inc."

None of the decision-makers I have spoken to, however, chose a fully outsourced support model due primarily to the criticality of data and the perceived inability of external staff to perform as well as internal resources.

Organizational changes take time to implement. If project deadlines are tight, it is prudent to avoid initiating large-scale, sweeping organizational changes prior to a project go-live. Generally, organizational changes are less critical at the time of implementation than the cooperation among team members and maintaining the status quo. Of course, in many environments there is no such thing as status quo, in which case there might be no better or worse time to restructure the storage support team. If this is the case with your organization, it is still beneficial to avoid timing an organizational shift to coincide with a large, revenue-impacting project.

Service Level Management

Next to ILM, service level management (SLM) is one of the most buzz-worthy storage terms in use today. As a concept, SLM is not new; many application and hosting environments have had service level agreements (SLAs) in place with their clients for some time. SLAs allow for the monitoring and measurement of performance and solution delivery over time. Without an SLA to fall back on, there is no concrete benchmark against which the implemented solution can be graded.

In many instances, application environments already have SLAs with their clients outlining application performance and availability. Likewise, many hosting organizations have SLAs outlining host availability and performance. Some environments might even have SLAs governing the storage attached to the hosts, but few are likely to have storage-specific SLAs for services other than availability.

Storage-specific SLAs are rapidly gaining acceptance as organizations seek to build and implement the storage utility model. Simply put, SLAs are the most critical piece of the infrastructure required to support the storage utility model.

The difficulty of building the processes required to support SLAs depends entirely on the overall IT infrastructure of your organization. Large organizations with many different services and client groups will find building an SLA framework from scratch difficult and time-consuming. The effort, however, will be rewarded. When an SLA framework is completed, execution becomes almost a formality. All new products and services must merely meet the values set forth in an SLA.

Defining the Storage Vision

Defining the storage vision—the goal of providing storage as a utility-like service—helps to secure the support of executive sponsors and outlines a basic roadmap for achieving the consolidated utility model. By now, this concept should be familiar to most IT professionals and many of the benefits of such a model should be obvious: cost containment, cost reduction, and improved service to name a few.

The view of the storage support team as internal service provider however, can be distasteful to some, and the astute client recognizes the next step after creating and implementing the utility model is billing (cost recovery or chargeback). This is a key concern of many application owners and consumers of storage, especially those who benefited from the obfuscation and chaos of the late 1990s when monitoring consumption rates and TCO was unheard of.

One concept that can be used to help navigate the implementation of the storage utility model in your environment is that of remuneration. When the cost-recovery concept is initially broached, if end users understand that, just as they can expect to be billed for their usage, they have recourse to financial recompense if the service does not meet the expectations defined and documented in the SLA, tensions are likely to be eased. It is a rare species that shies away from a money-back guarantee.

NOTE Financial impact and remuneration can be calculated solely on a TCO basis or, for external facing systems, as a percentage of revenue impacted (dollars per minute of downtime). It would be wise to ensure that the vendor providing services to meet your own SLAs is also bound by the same financial penalties as those facing the storage support team.

Another tactic to consider using to mitigate the impact of implementing the storage utility model is to create SLAs for a pilot project or service. This demonstrates to application owners and end users exactly what to expect when the model is fully implemented. A pilot project can help ease fears about your ability to support an SLA for storage as a utility as well as relieve clients' concerns over what the final product will look like.

If there is intense pushback against the storage utility model, it is also possible to implement the SLA framework and utility model without a charge-back mechanism. The SLA framework and utility model provide ample data for the purposes of measuring storage costs and storage performance. After the framework is in place, the ability to control costs and quality is at your disposal.

It is hard to overstate the importance of securing executive sponsorship for implementing an SLA framework for storage services and support. Without executive sponsorship, any program designed to implement SLAs fails. Without SLAs, the storage utility model will be hampered by indistinct and unclear objectives and any push towards measuring client usage and recovering costs are met with resistance.

The clients should believe that having SLAs protects their best interests as much as the storage team does. Just as it is critical for the storage support team to have an SLA defined with their clients, they must also have a clearly defined SLA with the storage vendors (if you use a fully outsourced models you probably already have an SLA in place with at least one party in the storage value chain). Indeed, each of the values should match so that the appropriate service levels are met for all parties and so that the storage team is not left in the middle without recourse to resolution between vendors and clients.

Defining the Services

After the appropriate executive backing is in place and clients have agreed to an SLA framework, it is important to clearly define each service that will be measured within the framework. It is not critical that every one of the following services are tracked and monitored, but it is likely that at least some of these are of interest to the end users and clients:

- Availability—Total uptime.

- Performance—Agreed upon unit of measurement (response time, IO/sec).

- Break-fix—Hardware and software troubleshooting and repair.

- Provisioning—Allocation and de-allocation of storage devices.

- Capacity planning—Projecting for storage growth.

- Financial analysis—Cost accounting and billing for storage services.

- Data integrity—Backup and restore.

- Other services can be built around disaster recovery and business continuance as needed.

It is quite likely that many environments will tend to build SLAs only around the first four of these services, especially if dedicated resources are already assigned to capacity planning and financial analysis. Obviously, availability and performance are two metrics that are easily obtained and are most often already covered in an SLA with the application groups and their clients. SLAs for these services will undoubtedly be requested by your application groups and should likewise be required from your storage vendors. It is also essential that storage, host, and application SLA values match.

How break-fix and provisioning services are handled depends on your choice of storage support models (virtual team, dedicated team, and outsourced services). If these services are performed by a separate entity (as in an outsourced services model), you should ensure that there is some type of contractual obligation guiding and measuring the delivery of these services, especially if you have agreed to financial remuneration for missed SLAs.

NOTE   The most commonly recognized authority on IT service frameworks is the Information Technology Infrastructure Library (ITIL).

Finalizing the Framework Repository

When the services are defined and the SLAs are finalized, it is important that the resulting documentation be stored securely and centrally for easy access. In the event of an outage it will be necessary for the end users and service providers to revisit the documented availability and recovery times originally agreed upon.

If the overall outage window has been exceeded or the availability number has not been met, a postmortem required to determine what, if any, recourse the clients and end users might have as part of recovering from the outage. If there is financial impact to consider, what portion of that is financially recoverable from the storage team? What portion is recoverable from the storage vendors? These issues, if not clearly outlined and documented initially, need to be revisited after each outage. It is critical then that the documentation is kept updated and that lines of communication between all stakeholders remain open.

Ongoing negotiations with stakeholders are required on a quarterly basis to review usage rates as well as fluctuating storage costs. It is essential that meetings be held on a regular basis between all interested parties to review performance metrics and to ensure that expectations are met.

Access to relevant documentation streamlines the process of reviewing availability targets.

Execution and Functional Roles

When the appropriate hardware solution is defined to meet the client's needs, the appropriate vendor is chosen, and the SLA framework is built, it is time to begin the task of execution.

There are four roles that are absolutely essential to the success of the storage networking project, regardless of the final form that your support structure takes.

Role of Project Manager

The first role is that of project manager or project lead. Even if your organization does not have a defined or distinct career track for project management, there needs to be a focal point for the complete operation from start to finish. The project manager is integral to facilitating communications between application leads, vendor representatives assigned to the project, and technical staff on the storage team. In addition, the person filling this role is responsible for clearing road blocks and ensuring that all deadlines are met. Budgeting, purchasing, and financial planning can be handled by this person if there is no dedicated representation from a financial analyst or purchasing agent. If you do not have a formal role defined for project managers, this presents an opportunity to senior technical staff members who might be looking for a career change. Professional experience managing projects is ideal; however, there is no substitute for corporate knowledge including an understanding of purchasing processes, change management and down-time policies, and application requirements.

Role of Storage Architect

The role of project manager might be complementary to or, in smaller organizations, encompass the role of storage architect. This role might be referred to differently in different organizations. Regardless, the storage architect is the technical lead for the entire project. This person should have a fundamental understanding of application architecture and operating system requirements for connecting to the networked storage architecture (FC SAN, NAS, and IP SAN).

Ultimately, a storage architect is responsible for designing or approving the disk layout on the backend, the design of the fabric in the middle, and the host fan-in to the switch. This person needs to work closely with the vendor to ensure that appropriate performance and design considerations are made when the vendor staff configures the disk array, and also needs to ensure that the storage administrator creates the appropriate volume and Logical Unit Number (LUN) assignments, and presents them correctly to the host.

For large environments, or large projects within smaller environments, it is almost essential that different individuals fill the project manager and the storage architect roles.

Role of Storage Administrator

The most crucial role to consider in the rollout of any storage networking project is that of the storage administrator. The storage administrator is integral to the ongoing success of the project. He or she is the primary contact after the project goes live and will more than likely be the staff member assigned to pager duty for the environment.

If you have created a virtual or a dedicated storage team, the storage administrator might be a junior staff member to the storage architect but might also have the most recent experience managing the systems and first-hand knowledge of the environment itself. Working with the project manager and storage architect from the networked storage support perspective serves to increase corporate knowledge and the capacity to contribute to other environments and new projects in the future.

NOTE The creation of a storage architect role offers career advancement opportunities for storage administrators who want to stay purely technical in their careers.

Role of Professional Services Staff

The use of professional services staff to fill roles outside that of direct product installation can pose some risks to the ongoing success of the project. Depending on the overall structure of your IT organization, handing off production support of your Fibre Channel or IP storage networks can prove difficult.

In addition to the significant cost of contractual support, there is loyalty and pride of ownership that comes with building and supporting your own solution. This is not to say that one solution is ultimately better the other. Rather it is important to understand that engendering responsibility and accountability is a lengthy and difficult process. An internal staff member who helps build and implement a cutting-edge, high-performance storage solution for clients whom he or she knows intimately, is more likely to respond quickly in the middle of the night when a critical piece of the solution fails. A contract staffer might also respond, but also bills by the hour and in some cases might not provide best-in-class support.

NOTE It is easy to find the financial break-even point for using external support staff over an internal dedicated team. The ongoing support contract should be a flat rate for the calendar or fiscal year regardless of the time of day or number of hours. If that is not the case, you must calculate an estimated hourly overage, preferably based on trending for the previous year's after-hours calls. Using that same number of hours for trending, calculate and compare the annual wage for the appropriate number of full-time employees while adding in any additional hourly rates for on-call pay.

Much has been said about the potential gains from using consultants and external professional services for storage installation and ongoing maintenance.

There is, of course, no substitute for a learned and experienced internal staff member intimately familiar with both the applications and the storage protocols in their own environment. If you do not have an internal support staff and you are starting from scratch, you might have no alternative than to use professional services, either from the storage vendor or from a third-party integrator or consultancy.

Building a storage support staff internally takes time; however, engagements with storage consultants can lead to opportunities for finding and hiring solid candidates, many of whom might be tired of traveling and willing to consider other options if they are not bound by a non-compete clause.

Professional services organizations, third-party integrators, and consultants can bring with them a wealth of product and project knowledge to enable the success of your installation. Vendors might also try to bring in inexperienced technicians and support personnel to increase knowledge and value to the firm (increasing their capability to book billable hours). Obviously, experience has to come from somewhere, but you have the right to not have consultants learning on the job at your expense. Before agreeing to a contract with a vendor or service provider, ask to review the resumes of the staff members being assigned to your account. It can also prove valuable in the long run to schedule an interview for potential candidates with your core team members to ensure compatibility and to cross-check knowledge bases.

Any engagement with a consultant or integrator must be bound by the agreements of both SLAs as discussed earlier and by a clearly scoped statement of work (SOW). An SOW serves as the spine of any engagement, and as such should outline clearly all deliverables and milestones. These deliverables should be mutually agreed upon, and a copy of the signed SOW should be provided to both the vendor and the customer project leads. The milestones in the SOW should be reviewed and should match the project plan for the overall project. If the milestones and the timelines do not match those of the project, the SOW is not properly scoped, and either the project or the SOW should be updated accordingly.

If you already have a large internal support framework and still choose to implement consulting or professional services, it is essential that you clearly communicate your rationale for doing so. It should be apparent that there are either knowledge gaps in your current support model that can be temporarily filled by using outside services, or that the long-term strategy is to have external professional services handle the mundane and dreary ongoing support tasks while moving your own staff into a more strategic role. Failure to communicate any changes in functional roles can lead to a crisis of faith in management and your leadership, and can raise the ugly specter of outsourcing. If the overall strategy for your firm is to outsource major initiatives, then that strategy should be broadly communicated.

The use of consultants in general, if not appropriately sold to your technical staff, can in fact lead to serious personnel issues. If there are incompatible personalities, your own staff might in turn refuse to cooperate with consultants (rightly or wrongly), derailing any progress on your project.

Conclusion

This chapter highlighted the value proposition of each of the technical solutions previously introduced in Chapter 2. This chapter also introduced the concept of oversubscription, the differences between a redundant and a resilient architecture, and the advantages and disadvantages of the two main SAN topologies in use today (core and core-edge).

This chapter also covered the "request-for-x" process, functional roles, service offerings, and the differences between support models (virtual, dedicated, and outsourced).

Although it is up to the decision makers in your organization to determine the usefulness and appropriateness of each solution and its fit in your storage support model, the data provided here should assist you in the decision making process. The ability to choose the right vendor and the right solution is the product of having the appropriate knowledge. This chapter illustrates that, as the storage vision matures, the vision enablers, particularly the technology and the people, become increasingly critical.

Chapter 5, "Maximizing Storage Investments," outlines what should happen after the migration, how to maintain service levels, and how to keep the TCO low across your environment. Ultimately, the question to be addressed is how to get the best performance and financial return from your investment in storage networking technologies. Fine-tuning the TCO is challenging, but the process is simplified by instituting storage strategies such as consolidation and recovery, and, as products and processes mature, by implementing an information lifecycle management framework.

References

[1]Everett M. Rogers. *Diffusion of Innovations*, Fifth Edition. New York: Free Press, 2003: p. 37.

[2]Ibid. p. 281.

[3]Moore, Geoffrey A. *Crossing the Chasm*, Revised Edition, 1999. New York: Harper Business, 1999: pps 10–14.

CHAPTER 5

MAXIMIZING STORAGE INVESTMENTS

The previous chapters demonstrated how to estimate and justify the financial impact of storage networking technologies in a firm. The deployment methodologies for staffing these projects and the overall support framework for managing storage networking products going forward are both crucial cost components. Ultimately, however, the true benefits of storage networking technologies are realized over the long run through decreased management and labor costs. Organizational changes and strategic planning carry these initiatives only so far. Fundamental process changes are also required to become a storage-centric business. Process change ensures the preservation and creation of value through fiscally responsible operations of storage environments.

Over time, advances in server and software technologies play a larger role in the administration and management of storage environments and enable companies to achieve increased utilization and economies of scale. This chapter provides a brief overview of a handful of groundbreaking products designed to lower the cost associated with hosting IT solutions through optimization and virtualization of computing assets.

This chapter also provides an overview of process changes required to manage storage costs after implementing a storage network. Special consideration is given to centralization, consolidation, and virtualization as guidelines for maintaining a flexible, robust, and easy-to-manage enterprise storage environment. This chapter also demonstrates how to manage storage costs within an Information Lifecycle Management framework.

Enterprise Storage Software

Enterprise storage software is critical to the success of any storage management initiative. Unfortunately for the end user, storage management software products on the whole are relatively immature. A brief overview of the market illustrates recent dips in revenue, and it indicates that additional consolidation (through mergers and acquisitions) might very well be on the horizon.

The overall storage software market, which includes backup software, disk management software, and storage resource management (SRM) software, as shown in Table 5-1, reflects a similar decline as that experienced in the disk market. Table 5-1 shows the worldwide revenues in millions of dollars for storage software and services.

Table 5-1 *Worldwide Storage Software and Services Market ($M), 1999–2003 (Source: IDC, 2003)*

	2003	2002	2001	2000	1999
Storage Software	$6621	$5730	$6157	$6113	$4640
Storage Services	$23,360	$21,171	$20,552	$19,501	$17,250

NOTE   In addition to the "lumpiness" of the software revenues, it is also critical to note the steady increase in storage services revenue. These figures indicate strong growth in the use of professional services staff to install, configure, and manage storage hardware and software.

In the long run, software revenue figures are augmented by the eventual maturation of storage management products, a process that is still, at least in part, dependant on consolidation in the storage software market itself.

BMC Software's exit from the SRM market (and subsequent sale of Patrol Storage Manager to EMC), StorageNetworks' flameout, and EMC's purchase of Legato, Documentum, and Astrum increase the chances that products on the market eventually meet customer requirements.

These developments also indicate that additional consolidation is still on the horizon. As is typical of the churn around the chasm, product adoption rates and product innovation rates are "lumpy," showing spikes and valleys until the cycle rounds off with the early and late majority adopters.

A primary factor of the recovery of the enterprise storage software market is the demand for SRM software. SRM software is a fundamental component of any storage management initiative and eventually the one tool most capable of maximizing storage investments.

Storage Resource Management

Storage consumers have undoubtedly waited a long time for SRM tools to make their lives easier. Until SRM products mature completely, which depends in part on the ongoing development of standards for storage hardware products, storage managers and storage decision-makers remain dependant on a combination of home-grown tools and reports for capacity planning and provisioning. The tools available on the market today play only a small role in the day-to-day tasks required for the management of enterprise storage. Many customers who have already purchased and implemented SRM solutions are still reliant on traditional spreadsheet solutions for making critical decisions regarding the purchase, allocation, and de-allocation of storage. For SRM software vendors, the major competition is not other vendors, but their customer's own spreadsheets and processes.

SRM tools have high price tags, are notoriously difficult to implement, and in many cases, they have not delivered the critical reporting functionality needed to replace home-grown solutions at the heart of IT storage departments. Integrating SRM solutions with these tools presents a significant challenge to customers who cannot deploy labor-intensive software agents on a wider scale until the replacement solutions match basic functional reporting requirements. After these requirements are met, customers still face scalability issues with products designed to gather enterprise storage data from each of possibly thousands of hosts. Consulting and professional services in the SRM space are currently poised to see increased revenue because many SRM installations either fail or they require significant customization to show value.

In the not-so-distant future, the enterprise storage software market will bear little resemblance to the entity we are familiar with today. Marked by intense competition, rapid consolidation, and significant advances in technology, the enterprise storage software market will become an oligopoly, with a handful of major players commanding the majority of the revenue. Over time, smaller companies, such as Boston-based Onaro and Silicon Valley-based MonoSphere, that focus on what are now seen as niche markets (for instance, predictive change management and virtualization) will gain momentum and market share by supplying unique features and functionality that lessen the burden of storage management.

Currently the SRM market is, with a few exceptions, marked by a handful of immature products that show significant promise.

Reliance on storage management tool suites, when they finally mature, will simplify every aspect of the storage yield, purchase, and deployment cycles. Capacity planning will finally move away from spreadsheets and utilization, at the disk level and application level (the allocation and utilization efficiencies) will be tracked in real-time through a GUI. Performance, service level management, workflow, and information lifecycle management functionality will also be built into future storage management software packages. Until that day, however, many customers are in a wait-and-see position with regard to installing the current releases of SRM solutions. Consequently, they must rely on de facto standards, homogeneous environments, and home-grown solutions to make their storage management and operational lives simpler.

Most capacity planning and disk procurement processes are based on a combination of historical trending, usage models, and guesswork. These inefficiencies, coupled with the immaturity of storage management software, irrational exuberance, and Y2K-related spending, are all responsible for much of the overcapacity and build out of disk capacity in the years previous to the most recent recession.

It is important to put the current state of affairs into perspective, however. If you concede that Fibre Channel solutions have recently crossed the chasm, and that IP-based storage networks have yet to do so, it is safe to assume that the storage world we live in today will be significantly different in a brief period of time.

Historically, storage management has been a host-based process. Truly scalable, truly sustainable storage management processes, those required for the creation of a storage vision, however, can be achieved only with a centralized management strategy. One of the companies currently working to change the storage management paradigm is CreekPath.

Storage Operations Management

Scott Hansbury, Chief Marketing Officer for CreekPath, agrees that a sustainable storage management process is achieved through a centralized management strategy. CreekPath, an independent software vendor founded in 1999, has been delivering storage and SAN management software solutions since

January, 2001. CreekPath currently offers an array of products designed to facilitate optimal storage operations management.

Hansbury believes that a holistic view of the IT organization and its infrastructure will prevail as the market for storage software management products matures. Products that can map critical processes and application functions to the infrastructure provide required services at every level of the storage value chain, anticipate customer demand, and will be successful in the long term.

Hansbury likens the current market for storage management software products to the market for office productivity software in the mid-to-late 1980s. Microsoft's capability to consolidate a disparate set of point products into a modular suite of solutions essentially disrupted an entire market.

Hansbury is also quick to point out that the original market predictions for office productivity software grossly underestimated the potential.

SRM is only one functional piece of storage infrastructure management, the first to see significant investment from storage software vendors. The remaining issues—policy, workflow, and automation—are currently being addressed. In addition, products that can map those functions from the application to the spindle, and are easy to install and use, will no doubt be the most successful.

Tools that provide the passive knowledge of storage resource data will eventually give way to software products that actively manage those resources. "Seeing the storage is not enough," Hansbury says. "Now it boils down to proactive management of performance and data (or information) archiving."

Point solutions on the market today address the passive and proactive pieces separately; in the near future, these products will be integrated to provide an enterprise view.

Mike Koclanes, CreekPath's Chief Technology Officer, views the evolution of storage management software as ever-expanding levels of abstraction layered on top of a guaranteed level of service, much like networking QoS (quality of service).

Koclanes believes that as IP-based storage solutions widen the choices for product deployment, the goal should be to limit the unpredictability of that service (with management techniques such as QoS). IO performance should be guaranteed to meet service levels as required, regardless of the dynamic nature of the choices available to the customer or client, and regardless of how the service levels are scoped (whether they are time-sliced, application-centric, or market-centric).

Koclanes's view eventually leads us to the need for an operations management system capable of matching available resources to required services. From a historical standpoint, the adoption rate of new, disruptive technologies is often underestimated. Koclanes believes that the adoption of centralized network storage management and the integration of Fibre Channel and IP storage network is no different. He believes that a single, integrated network that provides data services to both internal operations and external customers, and one that is capable of managing the security and billing for those services, is not too far off.

Koclanes concludes, "Software has to present itself as an application-centric networked service" to facilitate the same ease of use and interoperability in storage networking that has been achieved in computer networking.

The fact that interoperability between storage networking hardware components themselves and the software intended to manage that hardware has been insufficiently championed until now is indicative of the fact that component manufacturers have had only one goal in mind: decreasing time to market. Interoperability has been an afterthought at best with most hardware vendors, leading to dissatisfaction in the customer base. For storage networks to approach the same level of interoperability users are accustomed to seeing with LAN networking for hosts, significant energy aimed at standardization of interfaces is necessary.

NOTE Fortunately for storage networking consumers, a concerted effort is underway to do just that: standardize interfaces. The Storage Networking Industry Association (SNIA) was formed in December, 1997 as a non-profit organization dedicated to the advancement of storage networking standards through vendor and end-user collaboration.

In April, 2003, SNIA formally introduced Bluefin, also known as the Storage Management Initiative Specification (SMI-S), a specification jointly developed by industry leaders in an effort to ease the pain involved with managing heterogeneous storage environments. Storage networking manufacturers, such as Qlogic, StorageTek, IBM, EMC, HP, and others, worked together for almost a year prior to the announcement for designing and finalizing the specification, which is intended to alleviate many of the interoperability and management problems brought on by a legacy of proprietary storage networking interfaces. Having the Bluefin specification in place gives vendors an open standard to code against, which ensures that end users have products that play nicely together—a luxury that has up until now been completely out of reach for storage networking consumers.

SMI-S is based on Common Information Model (CIM), another networking industry joint venture designed to take some of the headaches out of managing devices on a network. CIM is an object-oriented schema and specification that simplifies and standardizes the interfaces necessary for gathering data from objects on a network and presenting that data in a useful format.

As the first organized effort geared toward interoperability and management, SMI-S offers potentially huge gains, especially for SRM and storage management software vendors and users of those products. One of the primary stumbling blocks for getting robust storage management software to market has been the lack of standard interfaces and schemas. Historically, each HBA, device driver, FC switch, and external storage unit has been designed in a vacuum with little or no effort made toward interoperability. The majority of storage networking and storage device manufacturers has accepted SMI-S as the standard interface specification. Although it will take some time to see products that use SMI-S on the market, after the specification is ratified, consumers will start to feel some relief. Consumers will then find it easier to make the transition from an application-centric to a storage-centric entity.

An application-centric user base is more liable to see storage as cheap and disposable, and although purchase prices have fallen, the management costs for storage have yet to see significant decreases, and the TCO for storage requires constant, active management to keep in line. The knowledge gap between infrastructure and application teams with respect to the costs of storage and storage management has never been greater. As the number of terabytes managed increases, only the storage management team is aware of storage as a depreciating capital asset, and not as a cheap and disposable tool.

It is crucial then that firms with significant amounts of storage installed (500 TB to 1 PB or more) become storage-centric entities in which storage strategies play an important role in the execution of management objectives, such as consolidation and business continuance. Application consolidation, storage consolidation, and business continuance strategies can be driven to success by storage-centric leadership, resulting in decreased costs and increased availability.

Cost-Saving Strategies for Storage-Centric Firms

Becoming a storage-centric entity requires executive-level sponsorship and active participation of individual contributors who foster awareness at every level of the organization of the value of storage as a depreciating capital asset with a corresponding yield and impact to the company's bottom line.

Reiterating the premise from earlier chapters, it is possible to drive significant change in an organization, from the bottom up as it were, by focusing on storage as an asset. Much like an EVA organization, a storage-centric organization views IT decisions with a focus on storage management strategies to ensure that value is created or at minimum not destroyed. Storage consolidation, server consolidation, virtualization, and Information Lifecycle Management—key initiatives in every storage-centric organization—can all be driven from the bottom up, given a viable, cohesive storage vision and active, executive-level support.

Storage Consolidation

Chapter 3, "Building a Value Case Using Financial Metrics," analyzed the financial benefits of a consolidation project, whereby Goodrich was able to eliminate $5,760,000 in maintenance fees by consolidating 80 external storage frames. The savings from maintenance fees were augmented by space savings in the datacenter, which deferred a $4,000,000 datacenter expansion project. In addition to resulting in fewer points of management, the consolidation effort provided a centralized agenda for lowering costs.

Consolidation is, of course, not without its caveats. The process of moving terabytes of critical data storage from multiple external arrays to just a handful does require significant foresight and planning to ensure that all high-availability requirements are met. A single, extended outage for several hosts attached to a 10- or 20-terabyte frame can affect large portions of a Fortune 500 company and virtually wipe out a small-to-medium sized business. Therefore, when planning a large-scale consolidation, it is critical that considerations be made for high availability and recoverability, and that the affected clients are aware of (and agree to accept) the possible risks.

NOTE	As consolidation begins to gain traction, environments are disturbed and many applications that had been forgotten are discovered. These applications might have less stringent requirements since their original deployment or they might not even be in use, at which point, the server and application can be fully decommissioned.
	The consolidation bandwagon will likely become something that disparate business functions want to get behind. Other teams will want to take part in the success of storage consolidation and will either support the initiative or start separate consolidation initiatives. Application teams might respond positively to a bounty system for recovery, whereby rewards are given for the most terabytes recovered or decommissioned. Business units might offer similar rewards for applications decommissioned.
	A storage-centric business strategy built on consolidation is capable of driving significant change in an organization.

Consolidation, a process marked by repeated planned outages to install HBAs and to copy databases, also requires considerable effort on the part of storage managers to ensure that disks are properly allocated and utilized. The process of dynamically migrating data to increase utilization and bolster operational efficiency is one that storage software manufacturers seek to automate.

Server Consolidation

Increased disk capacity translates into greater storage capacity in a single footprint. By the same token, increased processing power and decreased processing costs, along with advances in server and processor partitioning and management software, lessen the need for multiple servers and applications in order to do the same amount of work. Advances in operating systems software and processor architecture have made it not only feasible, but also cost-effective to implement server and application consolidation projects on a wider scale.

During the pre-Y2K era, processor sharing and server partitioning features were not widely available. Today, server partitioning is a widely accepted method of providing increased power and reliability to application environments. Logical partitioning at the operating system level allows for the dynamic allocation of central processing units (CPUs), offering the flexibility to meet changing project requirements. Hard partitioning at the server hardware level offers the capability to completely isolate from each other resources assigned to different applications within the same chassis. Although hard partitioning does have its own drawbacks in terms of flexibility, the capability to dynamically reallocate resources within the same hard partition is retained.

Equally pertinent to this discussion is the increased economies of scale gained by clustering multiple, smaller (or blade) servers as hosts to create server farms capable of providing highly available, efficient, and cost-effective processing power. The ability to scale horizontally, due to increased processor power, has all but replaced the drive to scale vertically. High prices for software and operating system maintenance drive many companies to adopt Linux and other open-source tools, whereas low-priced options for server infrastructure increase the use of blade servers for server farms (as mentioned in Chapter 1, "Industry Landscape: Storage Costs and Consumption").

In either case, the potential to provide increased availability to more applications at a lower price point is there. Regardless of the decision to implement fewer high-end server platforms or more low-cost servers, the decision to increase the application-server ratio is one that must be seriously considered to lower TCO over the long term.

The issue of risk versus reward raises its head in any discussion of consolidation, and server or application consolidation is no exception. The basic argument for server consolidation is easy to understand: Due to increased processor power, better fault management and load-sharing software, and lower costs, it is now possible to relieve the burden of expensive hardware maintenance costs by collocating applications on the same hardware. As long as the performance, availability, and uptime requirements can be met, then server consolidation, either to Linux farms or high-end servers, should be transparent to the application owners, with the exception of the downtime required to move the application.

Application consolidation is a riskier proposition and one that is harder to sell based on perceived diminished rewards. There are tangible benefits from using fewer software licenses required to perform the same tasks; however, despite the benefit of decreased points of management, the process of migrating and collapsing applications is much harder for businesses and IT departments to agree to than storage or server consolidation. Consolidation at the software level addresses the intricate methods that business functions use to interact with IT and with each other. Consolidation at the hardware level makes sense to many individuals because of the nature of computing advancement (Moore's Law) and the concept of an asset's useful life. Application infrastructure, however, reflects a company's proprietary knowledge whose wealth and value go far beyond that shown on the balance sheet. The primary issue of application consolidation is a question of business process engineering and requires a much broader scope of involvement across the enterprise.

This is not to say that application consolidation should be dismissed as a potential opportunity for lowering costs, but only that it should not be entered into lightly. On the one hand, the gains from a large-scale application consolidation effort can be significant, but it takes time, energy, and focus to turn them into a reality. Server and storage consolidation, on the other hand, can be sold as quick wins, which might spark some interest and initiative in consolidating applications. Consolidation at the disk, server, and application level ensures that the firm is capable of increasing the utilization of its assets.

Virtualization extends the concept of increasing utilization to the firm's entire set of computing assets. The ultimate goal of managing any resource is to achieve its maximum utilization rate. This applies not only to enterprise disk assets, but also to server and application entities. Unless there is a compelling reason to maintain a buffer of unutilized disks (or CPUs or switch ports), underutilization signifies waste. Tools designed to virtualize resources greatly simplify the processes behind management and consolidation, and therefore increase the utilization of those assets.

Virtualization

Although virtualization software packages are in the early adopter phase, the promise of virtualization of the CPU and the disk coupled with the capability to eventually shield system owners from storage and system administration pain (while increasing utilization) appeals to decision makers.

Host-based virtualization products have been in use in production datacenters for over a decade. Applications, such as VERITAS Volume Manager and Hewlett-Packard's Logical Volume Manager, provide transparency between the host and the storage unit to simplify the management of thousands of logical devices. These types of disk virtualization products are widely accepted solutions.

Network-based virtualization provides an additional layer of abstraction between heterogeneous storage and the hosts on a storage network, which eases the management of different storage platforms across the network. Virtualization at the network level increases application uptime by allowing resources to be dynamically allocated in the event of a planned or unplanned outage. Network-based virtualization also increases allocation efficiency rates by allowing devices anywhere on the storage network to be reassigned without impact to the application or the end user.

Companies, such as IBM and VERITAS, the first to bring to market intelligent virtualization solutions embedded on a switch, have set the pace of development with their releases of SAN Volume Controller and Storage Foundation for Networks respectively, and they will quickly erect barriers to entry to prevent further competition. Other types of virtualization products will quickly come to market to meet pent-up demand for virtualization functionality.

Early adopters of virtualization products find performance, reliability, and interoperability issues to be a factor, but for large environments in which the potential benefits of virtualization far outweigh the risks and costs associated with implementing immature products, virtualization is already making inroads.

As networked-based disk virtualization products mature, labor costs for managing storage across the enterprise decrease dramatically. Likewise, the virtualization of the CPU decreases the TCO for servers and applications. In addition to IBM and VERITAS, whose virtualization solutions are both available as separate service modules on the Cisco MDS platform switches, MonoSphere and Egenera are two more companies whose products are designed to virtualize and optimize computing assets.

MonoSphere

MonoSphere was founded two and a half years ago on the premise that corporate leaders facing dramatic growth in data storage would soon recognize the strategic importance of managing storage at the enterprise level and the need to address the rising TCO associated with managing heterogeneous storage with fewer staff.

NOTE   In February, 2004, I visited the corporate headquarters of MonoSphere, makers of cross-platform automated storage management (ASM) software solutions, to gain some insight on the storage software market, and to understand the effect MonoSphere's leadership believes virtualization and consolidation will have on the overall market for storage hardware. When I was at MonoSphere, I spoke with Ray Villeneuve, President and CEO, and Shridar Subramanian, Director of Business Strategy and Alliances.

Similar to CreekPath, Onaro, and other storage-related independent software vendors (ISVs), MonoSphere believes that future growth in the enterprise storage market is heavily tied to advances in software designed to manage and leverage networked storage. MonoSphere differentiates itself, however, from other storage software providers with the scale and scope of its flagship product, MonoSphere Storage Manager™ , which is designed specifically to automate tasks and policies that increase utilization of and lower the TCO for enterprise storage assets.

In April, 2003, the company began shipping MonoSphere Storage Manager™ for the Windows platform and, later in 2003, they shipped versions of the product for Solaris and Linux hosts.

MonoSphere is headquartered in Silicon Valley and has a research and development center in Tel Aviv, Israel.

The MonoSphere Storage Manager™ product is designed to provide a highly detailed view of the utilization of an enterprise's storage assets and to provide a methodology and toolset for migrating data to unused or unallocated storage, thereby increasing allocation efficiency and protecting the value of the storage asset.

MonoSphere Storage Manager™ virtualizes storage devices and allows the user to create virtual pools that can be allocated and de-allocated with little or no impact to the host environment. This abstraction of the storage device, as seen by the host, facilitates the use of a tiered storage strategy to lower the overall total cost of storage ownership. The simplification of implementing a tiered approach to storage helps customers avoid some of the interoperability issues associated with heterogeneous storage, thereby increasing purchasing power for storage decision makers.

From a single, out-of-band console on the storage network, storage managers can view reports showing true capacity utilization based on a fine-grained view of which storage blocks actually contain user data. This is in contrast with SRM products that cannot distinguish between storage that is allocated and that which is used. To act upon insights gleaned from these reports, storage managers either use prepackaged (canned) policies or they create their own policy-based rule sets to manage data layout across pools of free storage.

At the application server level, a software driver continuously monitors usage patterns, latency, and throughput, providing historical trending and assisting the environment's owner with ongoing policy refinement.

Intermediate volumes, known as MonoSphere Adaptive Volumes, are used to stage and destage data as it is moved between pools of storage by a separate, in-band server dedicated to the MonoSphere Storage Manager™ application. This server handles the actual data migrations between the unused devices, pools, and tiers as dictated by policies specific to the environment, and it minimizes the impact of the migrations on the hosts on the storage network. A common application for this unique capability is to create "spillover" storage that is used as local storage capacity becomes filled. In this way, local storage can be made to behave as if it were infinitely large, without impacting applications, so applications never outgrow their storage.

By simplifying the process of data migrations between tiers and by providing an accurate and up-to-date view of an environment's allocation efficiency, MonoSphere Storage Manager™ is positioned to radically change the way storage is managed in today's enterprise.

Egenera

Egenera, based in Marlboro, Massachusetts, intends to capitalize on the confluence of events and market drivers that it believes led to the next inflection point in the server market. Egenera builds the Egenera BladeFrame system, pools of massively scalable processing resources designed to meet the market demand for highly redundant, highly available environments. The nature of the blade computer, coupled with the virtualization of the IO components in the subsystem, means that the BladeFrame can lower the TCO by increasing the utilization of the processor much in the same manner as SANs increase the utilization of disk storage.

NOTE	In February, 2004, I spoke at length with Susan Davis, Egenera's Vice President of Product Marketing and Management, about server consolidation, grid computing, and the latest inflection point in the market for high-end servers.

Egenera was founded in 2000 by Vern Brownell, former CTO of Goldman Sachs, as an answer to the primarily physical problems he saw facing large enterprise datacenters. The traditional view of the server as an isolated resource, similar in concept to direct-attached storage (DAS), along with the need to provide highly-available computing power, has led to rampant growth of server islands that have become a cost and management nightmare. The proliferation of servers and storage in the datacenter, the increased points of management, and the related costs inspired Brownell to design a system capable of meeting performance and reliability constraints while reducing the number of managed resources in the enterprise. The end result has been a fundamental change in the concept of the server itself.

Server consolidation (or grid computing in a larger sense) is at a basic level about raising the utilization of the processor by providing sharable computing resources as a utility. Just as storage networking and storage consolidation is about increasing the utilization of the storage resources, processing area networks, such as those built by Egenera, increase the utilization of server resources by allowing groups of CPUs to be allocated to and de-allocated from an application's resource pool. The unutilized processors can therefore be shared between environments lacking resources, thereby offering investment protection and increased return on investment (ROI).

The virtualization of IO components in the BladeFrame creates a holistic view of the resources managed with intelligent software to make allocation and assignment of resources a painless process. Whereas in the past, the purchase, installation, and assignment of server resources in the datacenter involved the management of a number of different processes and physical elements, the use of blade farms to virtualize all IO components at the server level adds flexibility while reducing operational complexity.

This level of virtualization goes beyond the common concept of layers of abstraction provided by complex software stacked on top of numerous hardware entities. Egenera seeks to limit the number of IO entities underneath the virtual view provided by its management software.

Susan Davis believes that the inflection point in the server market is the result of the recent economic downturn, increased processor power, the growing acceptance of Linux in the datacenter, and, of course, customers' requirements to reduce acquisition and management costs while providing world-class technology solutions for their clients.

Egenera's successive years of triple-digit growth indicate that even though the grid computing concept is still in the early adopter phase, the market for solutions such as those provided by Egenera is rapidly growing.

Information Lifecycle Management

Instituting an information lifecycle management (ILM) framework, a process designed to guide the migration of data to different tiers or classes of storage as its usefulness declines over time, is a fundamental strategy designed to lower costs. As part of an ILM infrastructure, different tiers of storage with varying levels of functionality and availability are provided at different cost structures. As the value of the data declines over time, it is migrated to cheaper and cheaper disks until it is archived or deleted.

NOTE	Migration to storage networks and consolidation should be considered a fundamental step before initiating plans for instituting an ILM infrastructure.

As a holistic approach to IT infrastructure, ILM addresses the data itself, the kernel of intellectual property at the firm's core, and it weighs the value of the data against the costs of the infrastructure required to support it. In many ways, ILM extends the core-context debate into the tangible realm of managed terabytes: Core data is that which should reside at the uppermost tier, whereas contextual data can be transformed into a more manageable format or deleted entirely. In either case, it is necessary to determine the break-even point at which it becomes too costly and unwieldy to provide tier-one support for tier-three data. An example of this analysis is provided in the next section.

NOTE   Also keep in mind that the labor involved in implementing both SRM and ILM in your framework increases your TCO for the solution. Including the costs of the SRM and ILM management solution in the TCO analysis for your environment is required for an accurate portrait of cost trends.

Managing Costs in an ILM Environment

Managing storage costs for the life of the storage asset requires up-to-date and accurate cost data at each tier and across the enterprise. Few organizations have sufficient time and energy to devote to tracking and fine-tuning TCO data. Where possible, TCO initiatives can be driven by the storage team, but they are always reliant—at least to some degree—on asset management and purchasing data to provide granularity and accuracy.

To correctly position the data in the requisite tier, it is necessary to analyze the break-even point for managing that data according to its priority, business relevance, and revenue impact. For the purposes of this discussion, we cover only three tiers: a high-end tier (Gold), a mid-range tier (Silver), and a low-end tier (Bronze). Additional tiers can be created, although management costs increase as the number of tiers increases. In the following examples, the per megabyte purchase price is (inclusive of maintenance) $0.10 for Tier 1, $0.05 for Tier 2, and $0.03 for Tier 3. In addition, the following assumptions are made for each tier:

- The discount rate is ten percent.

- Future labor costs are discounted using net present value (NPV).

- One full-time equivalent (FTE) can effectively manage 1.5 TB.

- Utilization is ignored.

- Growth is stagnant.

- The depreciation schedule is three years.

- Cash basis is for all three years.

This section shows an example at each tier.

NOTE   It is critical to note that at this point in time, heterogeneity is key to gaining economies of scale, and management costs through a tiered infrastructure without the benefits of interoperability initiatives such as Bluefin, actually increase with the addition of different platforms into the support matrix. As hardware and software products mature and long-awaited interoperability subsequently materializes, then and only then will a tiered infrastructure be able to aggressively lower management costs.

Currently, hardware solutions for each vendor at each tier (low-end, mid-range, high-end) require different management interfaces and different support processes, hampering the ability to scale support for different platforms across the enterprise. Although products from the major disk vendors have Java-based or web-based GUI interfaces, there is no way at this time to manage, provision, allocate or de-allocate storage across a vast array of different storage solutions from a single console without a third-party product.

> The capability for a tiered storage infrastructure to increase supportability for hundreds of terabytes is wholly dependant on hardware interoperability and virtualization software. For the purposes of the tiered TCO discussion, the assumption should be that virtualization software as a mature product has been implemented and that the tiered solutions are transparent to the storage managers and the end users—a scenario that should materialize in production datacenters by 2005–2006.

Classifying Tiers Based on TCO

It is important to understand that migration from DAS to SAN or network-attached storage solutions (NAS) (and from a non-tiered to a tiered storage environment) invariably requires significant time and resource commitments. These migrations do not happen overnight. During considerable lengths of time, there might be multiple environments in place for the same application at the switch, disk, and host level. These duplicate environments increase the management, and hardware costs contribute to an initially higher TCO. Consolidation efforts also involve the creation of duplicate environments, which raise the hardware cost components associated with the consolidated environments. Over time, the costs decrease; in the short run, costs spike. The following examples should help identify the break-even point of TCO and tier application.

Tier 1 (Gold)

This example assumes the following:
- The environment uses a total of 1500 GB (including local and remotely replicated copies).
- The $0.10 purchase price includes all licenses and maintenance.
- The value of one FTE is $100,000.00.
- Installation costs are $0.01 per megabyte.
- Backups are taken weekly and twice daily.

NOTE   Note that for the cash basis analysis, the FTE costs are the NPV of one FTE over three years using a ten percent discount rate.

Table 5-2 shows the TCO for a typical Tier 1 storage environment. Note that this number is the TCO for the storage only and does not include the costs for server hardware or application licenses. Cost components are shown as both cash basis and depreciation basis.

Table 5-2   *Tier 1 (Gold) TCO*

TCO Component Tier 1 (Gold)	Total Cash Basis Value	Year 1 Depex Value	Year 2 Depex Value	Year 3 Depex Value	Total Value
Total Storage (MB)	1,500,000	1,500,000	1,500,000	1,500,000	1,500,000
Labor Costs					
1 FTE	$271,000.00	$100,000.00	$90,000.00	$81,000.00	
Training	$2000.00	$2000.00	—	—	
Total Labor	$273,000.00	$102,000.00	$90,000.00	$81,000.00	273,000.00
Acquisition Costs					
Storage	$150,000.00	$50,000.00	$50,000.00	$50,000.00	
Switches	$64,000.00	$21,333.33	$21,333.33	$21,333.33	
HBAs	$20,000.00	$20,000.00	—	—	
Cables	$15,000.00	$15,000.00	—	—	
Installation Costs	$15,000.00	$15,000.00	—	—	
Total Acquisition Costs	$264,000.00	$121,653.33	$71,333.33	$71,333.33	$264,000.00
Add In SRM/ILM/ Virtualization SW	$0.03	$0.01	$0.01	$0.01	
Backup Costs					
Total Backup Costs	$100,000.00	$33,333.33	$33,333.33	$33,333.33	$99,999.99
TCO	**$637,000.00**	**$256,666.66**	**$194,666.66**	**$185,666.66**	**$636,999.99**
TCO per MB	**$0.41**	**$0.16**	**$0.13**	**$0.12**	**$0.425**

NOTE	SRM and virtualization software costs of $1,000,000 spread over a 100-TB environment would be $0.01 per megabyte. For an environment as small as 500 GB, the contributions to TCO are negligible. Although noted here, these costs are not included in the TCO calculation for these environments. However, these costs would be included in the TCO for the enterprise.

This mission-critical environment is comprised of three copies (a primary copy and two replicated copies). The value of this data is such that the increased TCO that accompanies the multiple copies and the multiple backups is an accepted cost of the firm.

As the data matures, however, the value of the data can decline, and therefore might not merit the increased TCO. Aging sales reports and last year's intranet data might have less stringent replication requirements and might not require multiple daily backups. At this time, the firm can decide to move the data to the next tier. The same size of environment classified as a Tier 2 and stored on a Silver-level storage infrastructure has a significantly lower TCO.

Tier Two (Silver)

The same assumptions hold for the Tier Two (Silver) environment, with two exceptions:

- The environment uses a total of 1000 GB (one primary copy and one locally replicated copy).
- The $0.05 purchase price includes all licenses and maintenance.
- Backups are taken weekly and once daily.

The same 500-GB environment stored at Tier 2 has significantly lower capital costs, as shown in Table 5-3. Note that this number is the TCO for the storage only and does not include the costs for server hardware or application licenses. Cost components are shown as both cash basis and depreciation basis.

Table 5-3 *Tier 2 Silver TCO*

TCO Component Tier 2 (Silver)	Total Cash Basis Value	Year 1 Depex Value	Year 2 Depex Value	Year 3 Depex Value	Total Value
Total Storage (MB)	1,000,000	1,000,000	1,000,000	1,000,000	1,000,000
Labor Costs					
1 FTE	$178,860.00	$66,000.00	$59,400.00	$53,460.00	
Training	$2000.00	$2000.00	—	—	
Total Labor	$180,860.00	$68,000.00	$59,400.00	$53,460.00	$180,860.00
Acquisition Costs					
Storage	$50,000.00	$16,666.67	$16,666.67	$16,666.67	
Switches	$32,000.00	$10,666.67	$21,333.33	$21,333.33	
HBAs	$20,000.00	$20,000.00	—	—	
Cables	$15,000.00	$15,000.00	—	—	
Installation Costs	$10,000.00	$10,000.00	—	—	
Total Acquisition Costs	$127,000.00	$72,333.33	$38,000.00	$38,000.00	$148,333.33
Add In SRM/ILM/ Virtualization SW	$0.03	$0.01	$0.01	$0.01	
Backup Costs					
Total Backup Costs	$21,000.00	$7000.00	$7000.00	$7000.00	$21,000.00
TCO	$328,860.03	$147,333.34	$104,400.00	$98,460.00	$350,193.33
TCO per MB	$0.32	$0.14	$0.10	$0.10	$0.35

The value of this data is still likely to decrease, and over time might not merit multiple online copies and daily backups. The management team should then make a judgment call about whether or not to migrate to Tier Three, the Bronze tier.

Tier Three (Bronze)

With the Tier Three environment, the same assumptions still hold for the Tier Two environment, with three exceptions:

- The environment uses a total of 500 GB (one primary copy only) of NAS devices (no FC switch components are required).
- The $0.03 purchase price includes all licenses and maintenance.
- Backups are taken only once a week.

As expected, the third tier (shown in Table 5-4) has an even lower TCO associated with it, primarily due to the lower acquisition costs of the hardware. Less frequent backups and no replication also lower the overall costs.

Table 5-4   *Tier 3 Bronze TCO*

TCO Component Tier 3—Bronze	Total Cash Basis Value	Year 1 Depex Value	Year 2 Depex Value	Year 3 Depex Value	Total Value
Total Storage (MB)	500,000	500,000	500,000	500,000	500,000
Labor Costs					
1 FTE	$90,333.33	$33,333.33	$30,000.00	$27,000.00	
Training	$2000.00	$2000.00	—	—	
Total Labor	$92,333.33	$35,333.33	$30,000.00	$27,000.00	$92,333.33
Acquisition Costs					
Storage	$15,000.00	$5000.00	$5000.00	$5000.00	$15,000.00
Switches	—	—	—	—	
HBAs	—	—	—	—	
Cables	—	—	—	—	
Installation Costs	—	—	—	—	
Total Acquisition Costs	$15,000.00	$5000.00	$5000.00	$5000.00	$15,000.00
Add In SRM/ILM/ Virtualization SW	$0.03	$0.10	$0.10	$0.10	
Backup Costs					
Total Backup Costs (1 full backup weekly)	$3000.00	$1000.00	$1000.00	$1000.00	$3000.00
TCO	$110,333.33	$41,333.33	$36,000.00	$33,000.00	$110,333.33
TCO per MB	$0.22	$0.08	$0.07	$0.07	$0.22

Table 5-5 summarizes the TCO comparisons.

Table 5-5 *TCO Summary*

Tier	TCO Cash Basis	Depreciation Basis: Year 1	Depreciation Basis: Year 2	Depreciation Basis: Year 3
Tier 1	$0.42	$0.17	$0.13	$0.12
Tier 2	$0.33	$0.15	$0.10	$0.10
Tier 3	$0.22	$0.08	$0.07	$0.07

For a 500-GB environment with three copies (one production, one locally mirrored, one remotely replicated) stored at Tier 1, the TCO is $0.42. As the number of online copies and the number of backups decreases, the TCO decreases accordingly.

If the per MB revenue associated with this environment is sufficiently greater than $0.42 per MB to cover all labor and fixed costs associated with additional server hardware and application licenses required to store data at the first tier, then it is in the best interest of the company to store this data at the first tier.

For example, assume that this external facing application facilitates an average of five transactions per hour every day for a year for a total of 43,800 transactions. If the average sale for each transaction is $100, then the annual revenue associated with this environment is $4,300,000. The corresponding revenue per megabyte is $8.55. The percent of storage TCO to revenue is then 4.90 percent. If this rate of costs to revenue meets the corporate goal, then the extra costs associated with the additional hardware for mirroring and replication is well within accepted limits. The following breaks down the costs and revenue associated with this environment:

Primary data storage (MB): 500,000

Average transactions per hour: 5

Average transaction: $100

Revenue: $4,380,000

Revenue/MB: $8.55

TCO/MB: $0.42

Percent of costs: 4.90%

Another way to look at revenue and associated costs is in terms of availability. If this same electronic commerce environment hosts 100 transactions per hour at an average of $1,000 per transaction, then an environment that provides only four nines availability—99.99 percent—or 8759.12 hours per year, cost the firm $87,600 in lost revenues. Table 5-6 shows the number of minutes downtime associated with the percentage of availability.

Table 5-6   *Availability and Minutes of Downtime*

Minutes Per Year	Availability	Minutes Downtime Per Year
525600	0.99999	5.256
525600	0.9999	52.56

In this particular case, a Tier One environment, if properly architected, is virtually assured of providing 99.999 percent availability. The justification for the environment is then related to the company's overall hurdle rate.

Table 5-7 highlights the associated costs, savings, and revenue impact as a percent of the fully burdened costs of the environment. If the company's hurdle rate is 14 percent or less, then the Tier 1 solution is sufficient investment protection based on four nines availability. If the hurdle rate is above 14 percent or less, then the electronic commerce environment should be hosted on the Tier 1 solution.

Table 5-7   *Revenue Impact as Percent of Tiered Costs*

Tier	Fully Burdened Costs	Availability	Minutes Downtime	Revenue Impact	Revenue Savings	Percent
Tier 1	$637,000	0.99999	5.256	$8,760.00	$91,240.00	14.32%
Tier 2	$328,860	0.9999	52.56	$87,600.00	$12,400.00	3.77%

It is critical to understand that the fundamental costs associated with each environment and each tier are the acquisition costs of the storage itself and the labor costs associated with supporting the storage and migrating the data between tiers. In a heterogeneous storage environment that lacks requisite virtualization and ILM-based software to make management through the tiers transparent to the storage manager, costs necessarily increase.

NOTE	Labor costs are a key factor in keeping TCO to a minimum. As mentioned earlier, currently the primary strategy for keeping labor costs down is homogenous storage. Force-fitting a tiered storage strategy into any environment with immature management software products raises management costs, and therefore, increases the TCO. As the number of terabytes managed by one FTE increases, the per gigabyte cost of management decreases, a classic example of increasing returns to scale.
	At Cisco, as shown in Chapter 8, "Cisco Systems, Inc.," management costs for a homogeneous environment scale linearly, whereas management costs for smaller heterogeneous environments increases over time. As enterprise storage software products mature, however, this distinction will disappear.

Conclusion

This chapter showed how the TCO for storage environments is directly related to management costs. As the purchase price for storage continues to decrease, and growth remains constant or accelerates, storage management processes will remain dependant on home-grown tools and immature software products. Until interoperability becomes a reality and storage management software matures, labor costs will increase, unless the environments are homogeneous. The Bluefin initiative, along with storage virtualization software will succeed in lowering the overhead associated with storage management.

Storage-centric organizations can execute a cohesive storage vision to lower costs and increase operational efficiencies. A storage vision comprised of consolidation and virtualization initiatives (both at the storage level and at the server level) can drive change throughout IT to increase utilization of IT assets and reduce waste.

As storage software products mature, a sustainable storage vision will include an ILM framework for managing information through its useful life, which, in turn, will continue to lower the TCO for storage.

As the case studies in Part II indicate, few companies have fully implemented a sustainable storage vision. Most early adopters have implemented only select strategies (migration and consolidation typically), where need is most acute and impact, in terms of both ROI and operational efficiencies, is quickly felt. Migration to storage networks is the most important strategy any company can implement. Without networked storage, storage-centric management strategies (consolidation, recovery, and virtualization) will not be successful.

The following case studies clearly show that implementing storage networks offers true business benefits, primarily increased utilization and increased availability, which have a measurable impact on the company's bottom line.

References

[1] IDC. Framinghaus, MA, 2004.

—Worldwide Disk Storage Systems 2003-2008 Market Forecast and Analysis: Conservatism Persists, but Opportunities Abound, IDC #31663, forthcoming.

—Worldwide Storage Software Forecast and Analysis, 2003-2007, IDC #29983, August 2003.

—Worldwide Storage Software Forecast and Analysis, 2002-2006, IDC #27477, June 2002.

—Worldwide and U.S. Storage Services 2004-2008 Forecast: The Opportunity Shifts, IDC #31042, March 2004.

—Worldwide and U.S. Storage Services Forecast and Analysis, 2003-2007, IDC #28992, March 2003.

CHAPTER 6

THE CANCER THERAPY AND RESEARCH CENTER

NOTE   I first met Mike Luter, Chief Technology Officer at the Cancer
Therapy and Research Center (CTRC) in San Antonio, Texas, at
Storage Networking World (SNW) in October, 2003. At SNW, Mike
presented the story behind the CTRC's move to storage networks
and the remarkable success they have had using Internet Small
Computer Systems Interface (iSCSI) storage area networks (SANs)
in their environment.

Mike has been with the CTRC for over seven years, and in that time,
he and his team have been responsible for the entire IT infrastructure
including the build out of the corporate metropolitan-area network
(MAN) and local-area networks (LANs), the migration to storage-
area networks, and the CTRC's complex migration to Voice over IP
(VoIP).

In the spring, 2004, I spoke again at length with Mike regarding the
deployment of iSCSI at the CTRC and the ability of the leadership
team at the CTRC to solve the critical business problems associated
with maintaining and supporting highly available storage networks.
Mike and his team understand the value proposition of
IP-based storage networks and how it is possible, through the use
of storage networks, to provide business critical services while
simultaneously lowering the total cost of ownership (TCO) of the
storage solution.

In addition to fulfilling his duties as CTO for the CTRC, Mike also
serves as the CTO for the San Antonio Cisco Users Group and he is
co-chair for the board of technology for Northwest Vista College.
Mike is also a member of both the Cisco IPT Customer Advisory
Board and the Cisco Technical Advisory Board.

As demonstrated in previous chapters, the financial justification for migrating
to storage networks must be significant to secure funding and to secure support
from corporate stakeholders. Without political and financial support, an ambitious
storage networking project, similar in scope to the one the CTRC has chosen to
implement, stands little chance of success. As you see in this case study, the
financial justification for such an implementation is clear.

IP-based storage networks, and iSCSI in particular, offer significant cost advantages over Fibre Channel SANs by utilizing in-house IP networking expertise, as well as networking infrastructure that is typically underutilized.

This case study analyzes in detail the following concepts:

- Investment protection

- Utilization

- Metro clustering

The implementation of an iSCSI SAN at the CTRC highlights the impact of IP-based storage networking in the healthcare provider industry. The format of critical care delivery has changed over time, increasing the need for simultaneous access to patient data in multiple locations. Recent HIPAA legislation stands poised to make a significant impact on the overall storage and network infrastructure required to support multiple, secure copies of patient's vital records.

Executive Summary

The CTRC based in San Antonio, Texas is a non-profit organization dedicated to the practice of and advancement in cancer prevention research and cancer treatment. Since its inception 30 years ago, the CTRC has been a leader in cancer treatment and cancer research. The CTRC and the University of Texas Health Science Center at San Antonio together form the San Antonio Cancer Institute, a collaborative engagement between two world-class research and treatment facilities dedicated to providing top-notch cancer care.

The CTRC is a state-of-the-art treatment center that specializes in radiation oncology techniques, such as brachytherapy (an extremely precise method of targeting tumors with radiation), radiation therapy (X-rays), and chemotherapy (taking of chemicals orally or intravenously). The CTRC also offers diagnostic services as part of their Positron Emission Tomography (PET) imaging center.

In addition, as part of an overall expansion of facilities, the CTRC built the H-E-B Ambulatory Surgery Center in January, 2002, adding outpatient oncology surgery to their list of available treatment options.

In addition to offering compassionate, best-in-class healthcare, the CTRC provides a Wellness Center for ongoing and supplemental care. The Wellness

Center at the CTRC provides complementary and alternative therapy resources for patients and their families, such as exercise facilities, nutritional counseling, and music and humor therapy. In addition, the Wellness Center offers Yoga, Tai Chi, guided imagery sessions, and other classes in stress management techniques.

Finally, the CTRC also sponsors the Institute for Drug Development (IDD), a non-profit organization whose primary aim is to develop drugs for the prevention and treatment of cancer.

Although it is quite clearly a pioneer in cancer treatment, the CTRC is also a pioneer in the adoption of IP storage networks. The CTRC has built a networked storage infrastructure on iSCSI to increase the utilization and availability of its storage subsystems and to leverage an IP infrastructure to increase business continuance capabilities.

To store scanned data images for thousands of patients per year, and to make these images available for doctors and surgeons who must remain mobile at all times, the CTRC has chosen a networked storage infrastructure that relies on the capability of IP networks to provide data transfer over theoretically limitless distances.

To understand exactly why the CTRC architected their environment in this manner and to understand the business drivers behind the early adoption of iSCSI in the enterprise, it is essential to understand the host and storage environment at the CTRC, their workflow, and the nature of the applications they support.

Storage Environment

As patients begin their treatments at the CTRC, critical data and vital records are collected. As the patient progresses through his or her treatment cycle, data pertaining to dose distribution, treatment planning, physician consultation, and diagnostics are collected and stored through a series of applications.

NOTE Luter states that the effects of HIPAA legislation are just now beginning to appear, and that it is hard to estimate the exact impact the new health care legislation will have on their storage infrastructure.

Growth rate in storage capacity at the CTRC is currently directly correlated to the number of new patients seen each year. HIPAA legislation and the CTRC's association with the CTRC Institute for Drug Development (IDD), Title 21 Code of Federal Regulations (21 CFR Part 11) might in the near future create a spike in the amount of data the CTRC is required to manage.

In terms of the amount of data captured, by far the most resource-intensive area is the application of *positron emission tomography (PET)* technology.

Of the 13.6 TB of raw storage used by the CTRC, 3.4 TB is unutilized direct-attached storage (DAS). The remaining 10.2 TB is consumed by a mixture of extremely high-resolution *positron emission tomography* and *computed axial tomography* images (also known as *CAT scans* or *computed tomography [CT]),* and *magnetic resonance imaging (MRI)* data sets. When these images are combined to form a single file, the average size of each file is roughly 100 MB.

NOTE   PET technology is similar to both CAT and MRI scanning in that all three techniques create images of the patient's body for diagnostic and analytical purposes. PET differs from MR and CT, however, in that it is capable of measuring chemical and biological changes in the body's functions, which in many cases can assist physicians in forming a more accurate diagnosis earlier in the course of the disease.

To provide caregivers at the primary location and researchers at the secondary location the same access to always-available, mission-critical patient and research data (including patient image scans), the CTRC needed to configure and implement an architecture that was not only scalable and highly available, but also cost-effective. Using the Cisco SN5420 iSCSI router and eventually the SN5428, Luter and his team were able to share the Gigabit Ethernet link between the two locations with another mission-critical application, VoIP, over the corporate WAN. The corporate IP backbone is comprised of 11 Cisco Catalyst 4006 series switches, two Catalyst 4506 switches, and one Catalyst 4507 dedicated to Layer 3 traffic. This integrated topology approach allows the CTRC to have a highly available, converged network at minimal expense.

NOTE   The migration from a traditional PBX to IP telephony in 2002 saved the CTRC $50,000 in a single year solely in terms of telephony maintenance and infrastructure cost reductions. The impact of IP telephony on productivity has yet to be measured.

A mix of PC-based 1u servers in each location (45 in total), most running Windows 2000 Server, accesses the 6.1 TB of mid-range Clariion storage via what is commonly referred to as a *metro cluster*. Only changed data is replicated between the two locations and although this architecture does provide for some level of redundancy, Luter is quick to point out that the environment is configured primarily for high availability and not necessarily for business continuance. Critical patient data is kept synchronized between both locations so that both the doctors interfacing with the patients and the researchers analyzing the treatment data have the most up-to-date and accurate picture of the patient's health.

Figure 6-1 details the iSCSI infrastructure at the CTRC. In this example, redundant pairs of SN5428-2 Cisco storage routers in each location provide data transfer services of both patient image data and server boot data between both locations.

Figure 6-1   *iSCSI Infrastructure at the CTRC (Source: The Cancer Therapy and Research Center, 2004)*

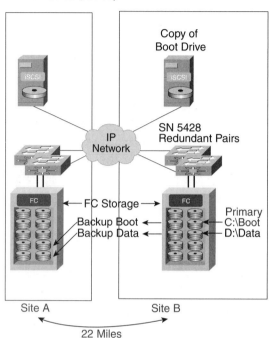

NOTE   At any given time, there is at most a 10–12 second delay between the two campuses on the MAN.

Although the need to carry large amounts of data across long distances was a fundamental requirement of the CTRC, long-distance replication was not the only reason iSCSI was chosen. The choice of iSCSI also reflected a concrete financial and business justification built on investment protection and TCO and return on investment (ROI) analysis.

The Move to Storage Networks

A number of business drivers precipitated the move to storage networks at the CTRC. Distance is the primary issue that drove the need for a networked solution to the storage management problem, as previously discussed; however, other solutions on the market could have solved the replication problem facing the CTRC, although with a significant increase in management and capital costs.

Initial Fibre Channel deployments were successful (Luter has utilized both Brocade and Cisco Fibre Channel switches to increase storage utilization), but without the use of the IP backbone to transport data across the MAN to the secondary datacenter, or without the purchase of an expensive SAN extension product, it was not possible to keep the data synchronized between both locations.

The financial and business justification for an IP-based storage network became clear after Luter and the management team at the CTRC analyzed the investment protection offered by an iSCSI solution. Considering the significant investment already made in an IP infrastructure for VoIP and WAN and LAN networking, and the capability to boost the utilization of the backbone infrastructure to avoid the costs associated with building a separate Fibre Channel network for extending the SAN, the rationale behind selecting iSCSI as a technology enabler is clear.

In addition to the bottom-line impact of implementing iSCSI, the use of network boot functionality over iSCSI provides ease of management for the 45 hosts on the network, all of which can boot from multiple boot images (for flexibility) and multiple boot paths (for redundancy) across the SAN. In terms of economies of scale, network boot via iSCSI allows the administrators in either location to apply patches and upgrades to the host operating system only once, instead of multiple times. In addition, having multiple copies of boot images available across the IP network offers an increased level of redundancy and flexibility for host management purposes.

Luter and his team clearly qualify as early adopters of iSCSI technology in the enterprise datacenter. The first implementation of iSCSI at the CTRC was built around the Cisco SN5420 storage router and began in 2001. Luter and his team migrated shortly thereafter to redundant SN5428-2s in both datacenters.

NOTE	Cisco Systems, Inc. announced the "end of life" of the Cisco SN5420 storage router in May, 2003. Although the product will be supported until 2007, Cisco encourages its customers to upgrade to the SN5428-2.

Most recently, however, Luter and his team purchased a Cisco MDS 9506 Multilayer Director SAN switch, and are currently in the process of migrating the environments from the SN5428-2 to Gigabit Ethernet IP Storage Services Modules on the 9506. Additionally, Luter and his team are evaluating the use of both iSCSI and Fibre Channel over IP (FCIP) as viable transport solutions for long-distance replication between both locations.

Total Cost of Ownership

Considering the nature of the environment at the CTRC (relatively small total storage requirements with moderate growth and high utilization rates), the financial savings associated with storage networking at the CTRC stem not from the migration of DAs to networked storage, but primarily from investment protection via the increased utilization of the IP network backbone.

With a mix of roughly 75 percent SAN and 25 percent DAS storage, and allocation efficiency rates of roughly 90 percent, Luter and his team stand to achieve only a relatively small ROI by migrating the remaining 25 percent DAS to networked storage or by increasing the allocation efficiency to 100 percent. For the time being, the additional 10 percent of unutilized storage is held as a buffer, the loss of which can cause a significant decrease in productivity.

The use of the Cisco IP backbone to transport block data between campuses boosts the utilization of the network infrastructure, which increases the value provided by networking capital expenditures; in this case, it is a pair of redundant Cisco Catalyst 4506s. In addition to storage support, the IP backbone provides transport for both voice and internetworking. Transport is just as much an asset as the storage components, and increasing the utilization of any asset serves to lower the TCO for the entire infrastructure.

Therefore, the addition of the SN5428-2 (to be replaced in the near future with IP Storage Services Modules configured on the Cisco MDS 9506) creates only a slight increase in the storage-related TCO, which is more than offset by the decrease in the overall TCO.

Including the cost of backups, which are completely tape-based, the TCO for storage at the CTRC is $0.036 per MB. Backup costs at the CTRC, based on a rotation of weekly, monthly, and incremental backups average just over $43,000 for a one year period and represent roughly 10 percent of the overall storage infrastructure TCO.

With only two staff members dedicating 40 percent of their time each on storage-related initiatives, and no contract or temporary laborers on staff, FTE costs for supporting the 13.6 TB of storage at the CTRC are relatively insignificant. Maintenance charges for the majority of the storage components are not a factor because most of the hardware is still under warranty and maintenance charges are reflected in the purchase price for the storage for the first three years of ownership. Raw storage acquisition costs then, exclusive of the Fibre Channel infrastructure (switches and host bus adapters [HBAs], are still the leading component costs contributing 51 percent to the TCO.

Network infrastructure costs, on the other hand, represent only about 2 percent of the overall costs. Although Fibre Channel components, including the Cisco MDS switch, make up 14 percent of the TCO, if the CTRC opted for a more complex and more costly SAN extension infrastructure, the costs would have more than doubled. In addition to capital cost savings, the CTRC also benefits from the lack of a learning curve associated with migrating to a different SAN extension solution. Because iSCSI traffic travels over the campus IP backbone, the storage network can be managed by the same networking team that supports the CTRC's IP telephony infrastructure, creating more economies of scale.

The chart in Figure 6-2 highlights the percentage each component contributes to the overall cost of storage infrastructure at the CTRC.

Figure 6-2   *Percentage Contribution to TCO (Source: Cancer Therapy and Research Center, 2004)*

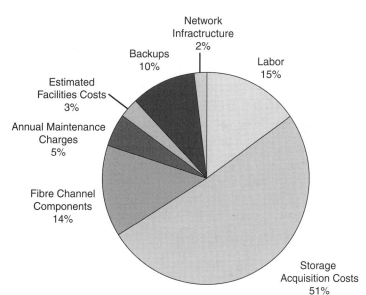

Future Initiatives

Over time, Luter and his team intend to create a tiered storage infrastructure with clustered Fibre Channel solutions at the high end and a mix of Advanced Technology Attachment (ATA) drives, optical, and content addressed storage (CAS) at the low end (with replication services between both campuses). Content addressable storage offers a flexible solution for large, image-intensive data sets whose frequency of access might be unpredictable, whereas optical data storage offers permanent and unalterable solutions for retention of large data sets.

The major IT initiatives on the horizon for the CTRC are completion of the migration to the Cisco IP Storage Services Modules (and decommissioning of the SN5428-2 storage routers) for both iSCSI and FCIP and clustering server environments for greater redundancy at the host level.

Conclusion

Analysis of the TCO of the storage solution at the CTRC clearly demonstrates creation of value on behalf of the storage and IT infrastructure team.

In addition to increasing the utilization of the IP network infrastructure already in place, the cost avoidance associated with not having to implement a costly hardware and software replication solution is significant.

The flexibility offered by iSCSI boot capabilities coupled with the implementation of ATA drives and CAS solutions will, in the long run, further increase efficiencies and drive down storage costs.

As the impact of HIPAA legislation on storage consumption is demonstrated over time, Luter and the CTRC might find it necessary to upgrade the size of the link between the two campuses. The backbone is currently sized appropriately to carry all voice and data between the two locations, but it is certainly not hard to imagine a time in the near future when HIPAA might cause this to no longer be the case.

CHAPTER 7

INTERNET SERVICE PROVIDER

NOTE   In the fall, 2003 and the winter, 2004, I spoke at length with the principle storage administrator for a major Internet service provider (ISP). In addition to discussing the frustrations with meeting client deadlines, getting a clear picture of total cost of ownership (TCO), and supporting a storage environment that has grown essentially out of hand for the last eight years, we talked about the feasibility of a storage utility model and the benefits of ongoing storage consolidation. His experiences form the basis for this chapter.

Although this case study is presented as anonymous, concrete financial figures have been omitted at the request of the parties involved. Financial analysis is a key component of any case study; however, the reader is encouraged to value the presentation of items that highlight other key concepts from Part 1, "The Storage Networking Value Proposition," namely the different methods that can be used to calculate TCO.

In this case study, significant gains from early adoption of storage networking technologies stem mostly from operational efficiencies (an increase in terabytes [TB] managed by the administrator) and from ongoing consolidations.

As noted previously, operational efficiencies related to flexibility and ease of management are difficult to quantify outside the terabytes per administrator metric, which includes measurable components such as the number, frequency, and duration of storage-related activities.

As of the time of writing this book, the total amount of managed storage at this firm approached 1 petabyte (PB). It is also important to note that this company has in common with many firms the desire to cut storage costs and increase operational efficiencies.

This firm has seen the amount of its corporate data storage reach staggering heights in the last three years. With two consecutive years of triple-digit storage growth, this firm makes an excellent case study in storage management strategies. As the company approaches the 1 PB watermark, it enjoys the privilege of over five years of experience with Fibre Channel protocols and devices in its datacenters.

As an early adopter of storage networking products, the storage services team at this firm experienced few of the same difficulties as other early adopters of storage area networks (SANs), thanks in part to previous exposure to Fibre Channel technology on Just a Bunch of Disk (JBOD) arrays. Some early successes were also due to the fact that the predominant operating systems in use at the time when SANs were first adopted were highly SAN-aware.

The storage services team seeks to cut costs and increase storage administrator efficiencies. These objectives are fulfilled primarily by a strategy consisting of ongoing consolidation and migration to higher capacity storage arrays, thereby addressing utilization on the supply side of the storage equation. The team is also building a reservation and request system that will allow it to accurately gauge consumption rates and ensure that unused storage is reclaimed, thus addressing utilization on the demand side of the storage equation.

Executive Summary

This firm is one of the largest providers of Internet access in the United States, providing both dialup and broadband Internet access to millions of end users.

After experiencing significant growth during the late 1990s and successfully creating new revenue streams by moving into new markets, this firm remains one of the leading Internet service providers. Currently, it battles for share of this fiercely competitive market with other Internet service providers, such as Juno and NetZero.

Storage Environment

This firm's storage services team supports storage for critical back-office applications including Enterprise Resource Planning (ERP) financials, Extracting, Transforming, and Loading (ETL) applications, data warehousing environments, Customer Relationship Management (CRM) applications, and multiple billing systems. The largest of these applications is a multi-terabyte Online Application Processing (OLAP) data warehouse.

All of the 900 TB of business data owned by the IT hosting group, and supported by the storage services team, is spread across a homogeneous mix of large- and mid-sized storage arrays. This storage is managed by a principle systems administrator and five other full-time storage administrators. In addition, the storage services team leverages the resources of a logistics specialist who focuses on reservation management and the ordering, shipping, and receiving of storage frames coming into and going out of the datacenter.

Roughly 80 percent of the 900 TB is hosted on multiple models of external RAID arrays from the storage team's primary storage vendor, the overwhelming majority of which (approximately 750 TB worth) is SAN-attached. The remaining 50–100 TB of data resides on mid-sized arrays, which are also Fibre Channel SAN-attached. Less than 10 percent of the overall storage is direct-attached.

NOTE   The data stored on the mid-sized arrays is for the most part less critical than that stored on the high-end arrays. Examples of this type of data are database dumps and archived data sets for various applications.

Because the majority of storage is SAN-attached, the storage services team is acutely aware of the connectivity cost conundrum involved with migrating a massive number of smaller hosts to a Fibre Channel SAN. In this scenario, a host might cost only $2000, whereas the FC host bus adapters (HBAs) required to attach the host to the disk might cost over $1000. This is a painful point for storage managers, but application owners and the business stakeholders who own the data reason that as the analysis proceeds through the storage value chain to the point where a single host can consume several thousand dollars worth of disk, HBA costs are negligible. They theorize that as the connectivity costs become a smaller fraction of the TCO, the investment in FC HBAs is justified.

The storage services team, which provides application teams a more granular view of storage TCO, is analyzing the possibility of using cheaper HBAs or utilizing TCP Offload Engines (TOE cards) to connect smaller, cheaper hosts to cheaper disks using Internet Small Computer Systems Interface (iSCSI). FC HBA prices are in fact falling, but not fast enough to make a financially compelling argument against an iSCSI solution for appropriate applications in the short-term. In addition, as the cost of hosts and CPUs continue to decline, the increased costs associated with TOE cards makes them less attractive.

The Move to Storage Networks

The first SAN at this firm was built in April of 1999, long before the creation of a dedicated storage support team, and long before many firms had even considered using Fibre Channel SAN technology in production environments. Rather than just move a small test environment to a SAN infrastructure, however, the storage services team decided instead to tackle one of the largest data warehouse environments, which at the time approached 30 TB in size.

The resulting data warehouse SAN was comprised of 10 small, 16-port fixed switches, 12 of the largest hosts, and approximately 10 external storage arrays.

Behind this decision to build a Fibre Channel SAN was a critical business driver: the need for flexibility.

Ease of use for provisioning large amounts of data is a fundamental component of operational efficiency. To increase the number of TB managed by an individual storage manager, the need to quickly provision storage for rapidly growing environments became a prerequisite. The data warehouse environment in which the first SAN was implemented was growing quickly with an estimated 2 TB added every six months. Because the environment was direct-attached Small Computer Systems Interface (SCSI), adding new disks required long outages, which could not be done during the day due to system availability requirements. The migration of the data warehouse to a Fibre Channel SAN gave the team the advantage of adding storage on an ad hoc basis to meet rampant and often unpredictable growth demands.

An additional driver behind the migration to SAN storage was the need for solid, first-hand exposure to what the team believed would ultimately become the new standard for storage deployments. Although many of the system administrators had already been exposed to Fibre Channel protocols while deploying smaller Fibre Channel Arbitrated Loop (FC-AL) JBOD devices, management believed that it was crucial for the remainder of the staff to become experts quickly in what would inevitably become a heavily-leveraged technology.

In particular, senior staff wanted to familiarize themselves with switched Fibre Channel ahead of the mainstream adoption curve so that they could better understand how performance and interoperability issues might affect their environments.

Interoperability of Storage Solutions

Although this firm certainly falls into the early adopter categorization for Fibre Channel switches, it is interesting to note that the storage services team faced few of the same tribulations as other early adopters (in particular, interoperability issues with products from various HBA and disk vendors). Because the operating systems in use at the time had strong support for Fibre Channel, the system administrators were able to make the jump from FC-AL to switched Fibre Channel with little difficulty. The team's earlier experiences with FC-AL technology coupled with the operating systems' capability to easily integrate with switched Fibre Channel allowed the group to sidestep many of the problems familiar to users of operating systems with weaker support for Fibre Channel.

The cutovers in the FC-AL environments, which had already utilized World Wide Names (WWNs) (the method of identifying objects on a SAN fabric), were smoother than the typical parallel SCSI migration to Fibre Channel. In such circumstances, HBA compatibility and interoperability issues were minimized by the early adoption of Fibre Channel.

Networked Storage Implementation

The current SAN implementation, which has grown considerably since 1999 from 10 16-port fixed switches to over 100 switches total (comprised of a mix of 16-, 32-, and 128-port switches), now hosts almost all of the organization's mission-critical data. These switches make up multiple fabrics in redundant configurations for a total of over 2000 SAN ports. The FC fabrics themselves are location-based, similar to typical IP networks. Each datacenter is divided into multiple raised floor rooms, and each room hosts its own redundant, dual-fabric SAN. Over time, the storage services team expects to see the fabrics in each datacenter connected via SAN extensions; however, currently the environments remain separate and distinct in an effort to limit the impact of propagated errors. For now, the architecture remains a collection of tiered fabrics with no distinct core and no distinct edge.

Tiered Storage Implementation

To lower costs, the storage services team implemented a three-tiered storage architecture. At the high end are the typical large, high-performance arrays with single or multiple FC fabrics as needed for redundancy. In the middle are the same high-performance arrays or mid-sized arrays configured without redundant switch fabrics. At the low end, Serial ATA (SATA) drive arrays are provided for large data sets that are written once and rarely read. Environments that fall into this category are low criticality applications with minimal performance requirements or database dumps that are used to quickly recreate databases in the event of data loss or corruption.

The use of approximately 200 TB of SATA drives since the second quarter of 2003 has made a significant financial impact, saving a large amount of money in terms of immediate cost avoidance. Large, high-performance arrays previously utilized for these types of applications were released to be used for applications with higher IO performance requirements.

SATA disk drives have an acquisition cost of approximately one-third or less than typical external array drives, and if used appropriately, management costs are minimized. The decreased mean time between failure (MTBF) of SATA drives typically scares off some decision makers; however, using these devices in a RAID or mirrored configuration and for less IO-intensive applications should offset the costs associated with a higher failure rate. In addition, data with lower availability requirements can be offline on occasion making the choice for SATA drive-based arrays ideal, as long as corresponding service level agreements (SLAs) are accordingly adjusted.

Even though the storage services team has built a tiered infrastructure, the team is not currently implementing solutions as part of a broader Information

Lifecycle Management (ILM) strategy. For the foreseeable future, the team plans to stick with the current architecture, whereby data with the highest availability requirements are hosted on redundant, dual-fabric SANs with multiple, replicated copies of the data stored on large, high-performance storage arrays. Applications or data sets with more modest availability and uptime requirements are stored on SATA drives. Data whose requirements fit in between are hosted on dual fabrics and large or mid-sized arrays with no replication.

The storage services team believes that today the costs associated with implementing a more rigid ILM framework and managing heterogeneous storage across the enterprise outweigh the benefits. Accordingly, there are currently no plans to utilize network-attached storage (NAS) storage to build out additional tiers.

NOTE   There are plans, however, to utilize NAS storage for office-automation applications and user home directories, but those environments are not managed by the storage services team.

The storage services team concedes that currently client SLAs are poorly documented and that the few SLAs that are documented do not explicitly state a client's expected availability in terms of percentages. Although these SLAs are not rigid devices to be used to adjust charge-back schedules, they are well established agreements between parties that document which applications reside on what type of storage and which applications receive priority status.

As far as charge-back is concerned, the storage services team knows approximately how much storage their clients consume; however, the mechanism required to do a complete departmental charge-back has not been fully developed. The storage services team is currently updating the request and reservation systems and plans to move to a full charge-back system by the end of 2004.

To execute this initiative, the team needs access to accurate and up-to-date TCO and utilization data, which is difficult to come by. In the absence of these numbers, however, the storage services team can adjust storage cost estimates based on the storage lease schedule, which sees frames regularly rotating out of the datacenter as leases expire.

Storage TCO

The storage services team has an estimate of the overall TCO per MB: It is a floating number that depends primarily on the number and frequency of backups and, obviously, administrator efficiencies. With six individuals supporting approximately 180 TB each, and with data storage still growing, the team continues to push the limit of TB per administrator supported.

The storage services team uses a home-grown spreadsheet solution to model storage usage and associated costs, but with costs continually fluctuating and the number of storage frames onsite changing weekly, determining an exact TCO number is often a futile exercise. To get a more accurate picture of TCO, new incoming arrays and old outgoing arrays are added and removed from the spreadsheet as soon as possible. Therefore, the spreadsheet solution is a valuable tool for capacity planning and analysis. Each individual environment must be analyzed separately to determine the actual TCO per MB, but for the purposes of discussing an enterprise-wide cost model, the generalizations are worthy of a closer look.

The most enlightening part of the analysis is the fact that backups are by far the most expensive cost component of the storage TCO. Like most TCO calculators, the team's model accounts for the costs of datacenter floor tiles, utilization efficiencies, Full-time Equivalent (FTE) labor, hardware and software acquisition costs, and the cost of backups. The team also factors in the costs of tape retention for multiple years. If you factor in numerous backups of multi-terabyte environments and include retention periods of up to seven years for some data sets, backup costs become significant.

NOTE   It is worth noting that a TCO that includes the costs of seven-year tape retention is significantly higher than the typical one-year snapshot of TCO. Both models are effective mechanisms for calculating the TCO for storage; however, a seven-year TCO model is better for estimating the value of the data that is stored on tape. The seven-year model (and the associated costs of backups) also leads one to believe that there is potential return on investment (ROI) to be achieved by adjusting tape retention policies and by archiving less critical data.

Ultimately, there is no one right way to model storage TCO. Either method, as long as it provides value to the firm, is appropriate.

In summary, backups represent over 80 percent of the cost structure for storage in the IT hosting environment. Hardware and software acquisition costs are only 10 percent of the TCO, and FTE time is only 3 percent. Approximately 1 percent of the total cost is attributed to the datacenter and facilities expenses (power, cooling, and floor space). The TCO cost components are illustrated in Figure 7-1.

Figure 7-1   *TCO Components*

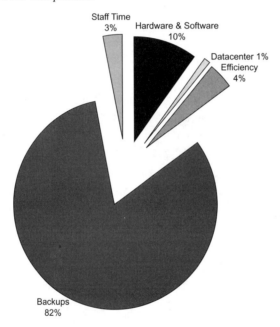

If the TCO is recalculated to include backup retention costs for a single year only, the portion of storage TCO that is attributed to backups drops below 60 percent. The retention-adjusted TCO components are shown in Figure 7-2.

Figure 7-2   *Retention-Adjusted TCO Components*

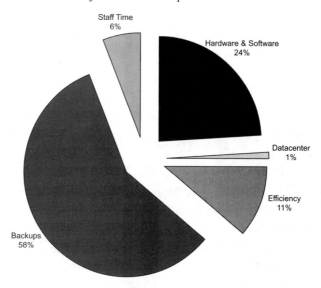

Supplemental headcount is provided as a service by the team's primary storage vendor. This additional labor is accounted for in the storage hardware acquisition costs. The additional resources increase staff efficiencies by at least five percent and subsequently increase the number of terabytes effectively managed by each storage manager. Operational efficiency is also increased by consolidation, which decreases the number of storage devices that require management.

A key element of the TCO model used by the storage services team is the outline of the storage life cycle, or the workflow that governs the procurement, configuration, deployment, and decommissioning of storage devices. The storage life cycle includes weighting factors for the number of groups and individuals whose time and efforts are consumed at each stage of an asset's useful life. Between the time a storage array is leased and the time it is decommissioned, individuals from 11 different teams are engaged to perform one or more tasks associated with the 14 stages of the storage life cycle. The weights are then used to establish a value for FTE resources consumed.

NOTE   It is critical to differentiate between a storage life cycle and ILM. The storage life cycle, as outlined in this case study, refers specifically to the various stages of the storage asset's useful life, and the amount of labor associated with each stage.

Instead of doing one large consolidation project each year, the storage services team performs rolling consolidations, which keep the overall costs down (and which keep the storage team fully utilized throughout the year). By using a leased storage model, the storage services team realizes the benefits of consolidation without incurring additional depreciation during the migrations when duplicate environments are temporarily created.

NOTE   The key benefit of a leased storage model is that a leased asset incurs no depreciation expense. Depending on the timing of payments, however, additional leased units for consolidation can increase the operational run rate in the short term.

For environments that have more than 500 TB, the depreciation expense for duplicate environments can be significant. For example, if 30 3-TB frames are consolidated to four 20-TB frames, and the migration for half of the data is estimated to take at least three months, then the additional depreciation expense during the migration (when the new assets would remain unused) would approach 10 percent of the total capital cost. In this scenario, a leased storage model avoids the expense associated with increased depreciation.

The workload for team members involved in a massive consolidation effort can become unmanageable in the short term. Ultimately, the decision about how often and how much to consolidate is up to the team and the team's management.

Replication

All of the business-critical 900 TB is spread across four datacenters.

Dark fiber between five metro-area endpoints, including the four datacenters and a metropolitan-area network point-of-presence (MAN POP), provides connectivity for Fibre Channel (FC) over Dense Wave Division Multiplexing (DWDM) and for data replication. A portion of the replication is continuous, but the majority of the copies are done with simple sync-and-splits over the wire either nightly or during business hours, depending on performance requirements and the availability of application downtime windows. For example, the ETL and data warehouse applications are read-only for most of the day and that data is synchronized at night when the daily data load processes are completed. Financial and CRM applications are also typically copied after business hours when utilization periods for these systems are low.

According to the storage services team, it is prepared for typical disaster recovery scenarios (weather events being the most common), with the most critical data being copied frequently enough between the multiple regional datacenters to allow for quick recovery and optimal business uptime.

Organizational Impact

From the inception of the first SAN until mid-2002, system administrators performed storage support duties on a strictly ad hoc, server-centric basis. Prior to the creation of the storage services team, systems administrators handled storage provisioning requests as a part of their daily activities.

In November, 2002, the dedicated storage support team, currently comprised of six full-time storage administrators, was formed to focus specifically on the ongoing consolidation efforts and other storage-related initiatives. Working almost full-time on consolidation efforts to reduce points of management, increase utilization efficiencies, and conserve datacenter resources, the storage services team directly addresses storage supply issues by managing the storage inventory onsite.

As the storage support processes mature, the storage services team is better prepared to outline in specific detail how much storage each application group consumes. The team admits, however, that it is not its policy to police storage consumption, but only to point out the details of application usage and let the application managers decide whether or not their teams are using the resources appropriately.

This is not to say that the storage team can ignore capacity planning because in fact, this is one of their primary roles. However, the actual question of monitoring storage demand is more of a managerial activity than a technical one.

Capacity Planning and Utilization

For the most part, capacity planning is done as much by feel as by equation. Internally developed tools and spreadsheets play a significant role in the capacity planning process, as does the corporate knowledge embodied by the storage services team.

Like storage administrators and capacity planners at other companies, the storage services team at this firm has difficulty estimating space requirements and timelines for new projects and applications, especially when the application owners themselves are not sure of the details. Fortunately, as other companies with major consolidation initiatives are finding out, consolidation projects are easy to justify based on increasing disk drive capacity and decreasing storage costs. Unfortunately, even as allocation efficiency improves as a function of consolidation, storage demand remains unchecked and utilization efficiency remains poor.

The use of a leased acquisition model requires disk arrays to be returned to the vendor when the lease expires offering the firm an opportunity to upgrade to the newest storage platforms. The increases in storage density work in the customer's favor because they are now able to replace 10 3-TB raw capacity frames with two 20-TB raw capacity arrays for less money than they currently pay in maintenance. In addition, they can still provide a 10-TB cushion as a spare pool for new requirements.

In some cases, past performance is a good indicator of future consumption rates. If an application's disk usage has grown at a steady clip of 15 percent to 20 percent per month for six months or more, it is a safe bet that it will continue to do so. In the team's environment, high visibility projects with unpredictable growth rates might need their own distinct storage buffers to ensure that the SLA for each application is continually met.

Because the acquisition cycle for new hardware is several months long (allowing for manufacturing lead times and procurement), the free storage pool tends to come in handy for supporting surprise projects and those environments in which the consumption rates spike unpredictably.

The storage services team still lacks an off-the-shelf solution for capacity planning, and although they have access to a storage resource management (SRM) application, the data from the application is not granular enough to serve as a planning tool for procurement purposes.

SRM

Although the firm does have SRM software installed, storage administrators do not use the application for the purpose of planning or provisioning new storage.

In an unfortunate circumstance for many SRM customers, some SRM applications on the market today (including the one used by this firm) are not yet capable of providing storage management data for Linux hosts. With 20 percent of the more than 1200 open systems hosts at this firm being Linux, storage administrators already have to log directly into each Linux host to retrieve important and meaningful data related to daily allocation and de-allocation processes. This scenario, of course, will be rectified as SRM products mature and are updated to include host agents for Linux.

Future Initiatives

Of the major IT initiatives currently underway, the one most talked about, after the migration of all storage to collapsed SAN fabrics, is the ongoing Linux rollout. In a partnership with Egenera, the IT hosting department plans to aggressively deploy "processing area networks" using the Egenera® BladeFrame™ System, a rack of blade servers clustered together to form a virtualized pool of computing resources. The storage services team estimates that by the end of 2004, the firm will likely double the number of Linux hosts deployed with multiple rollouts of Egenera® systems, most going directly onto SAN fabrics, thus lowering the overall TCO for the environment while at the same time increasing the flexibility of the storage support model.

Conclusion

The storage services team at this firm has demonstrated that storage-centric leadership can effectively lower cost structures for IT departments while still meeting and even surpassing client expectations for availability, reliability, and performance. This team has also proven that early adoption of new technologies does not always translate into headaches and heartburn. Instead, early adoption of disruptive technologies can in some cases accelerate the creation of value for the enterprise.

Consolidation has increased the operational efficiencies of the storage services team by reducing the number of points of management, while at the same time, the wholesale migration to storage networks has increased allocation efficiency. While these successes speak for themselves, it is critical to remember that at the heart of these successful implementations is the hard work of a handful of individuals.

CHAPTER 8

CISCO SYSTEMS, INC.

NOTE   I have been fortunate to be a part of IT hosting and infrastructure at Cisco Systems, Inc. for almost six years. As a senior systems administrator for the Enterprise Resource Planning (ERP) team between the years 1998 and 2001, I supported the day-to-day operations of the most critical hosts and databases at Cisco.

I joined the IT storage team in January, 2002 as one of two full-time project managers for a matrix support organization of nine individuals who spent anywhere from 20 to 100 percent of their time managing storage.

In 2002, the Cisco storage inventory was assumed to be 750 terabytes (TB) of raw storage, although we had no way of knowing the exact total. We had no fool-proof way of tracking storage frames or switches on the datacenter floor and no reliable way to estimate costs associated with any of our services.

In early 2002, the amount of storage attached to a storage area network (SAN) was approximately one fourth of the total storage. Since 2002, overall data storage has almost doubled, and of that storage, the percentage attached to a SAN has almost tripled.

In the past two years much has changed. The support infrastructure has changed drastically and there are now solid estimates for both inventory and fully-burdened costs. In addition, Cisco has entered the highly competitive SAN switch market with its own MDS 9000 product line.

As the adage goes, the more things change, the more they stay the same. Indeed, storage growth continues to increase. The migration to a Fibre Channel SAN platform (pre-MDS) was plagued by interoperability issues and immature products, a familiar situation for most early adopters of Fibre Channel (FC) technology.

The Cisco storage story differs from that of many end users only by degrees. As of December 31, 2003, the total number of managed TB at Cisco was 1460, or almost 1.5 petabytes (PB) of raw storage. By July, 2004, the total amount of managed storage had grown to over 2 PB.

Migration to SANs is the primary storage strategy at Cisco upon which hangs every other critical initiative (consolidation, recovery, and virtualization). The business benefit of moving to SANs is significant: a 20 percent increase in allocation efficiency, a reduction in maintenance expenses of approximately $5,000,000 per year, and an increase in operational efficiencies to 250 managed TB per storage administrator.

These successes are outlined in greater detail in this case study.

The IT department at Cisco has for many years focused on deploying cutting-edge solutions while maintaining operational excellence—two strategies that always seem at odds with each other. The triple-digit growth rate of data storage has done little to mitigate the challenges of early adoption of Fibre Channel storage solutions, which began in the high-profile ERP environment in 1998. The rapid adoption of the new Cisco MDS 9000 SAN switches indicates a shift toward early adoption of innovative products as part of an overall strategy to achieve a vision of a consolidated storage utility model—the ability to provide storage as a utility-like service—that was outlined almost three years ago.

This case study underscores the functional requirements that continue to drive the need for new solutions to storage problems. It is debatable whether Cisco, as builders of innovative networking solutions, is more predisposed to early adoption of new products than other companies. However, it is a fair statement to say that those more familiar with the advantages and disadvantages of new technologies are more likely to implement them faster than counterparts with less exposure to innovation.

Much like the other businesses analyzed in this book's case studies, the willingness to deploy new storage solutions and the ability to architect scalable, best-in-show environments rests squarely on the shoulders of a handful of knowledgeable (and typically overworked) individuals.

Executive Summary

Cisco Systems, Inc. is the largest manufacturer of computer networking devices in the world. With revenues of over $18 billion in both fiscal years 2002 and 2003, Cisco continuously leads the market for routing and switching hardware.[1]

Since it became a public company almost 15 years ago, Cisco has broadened its product line from pure-play LAN switching devices to a diversified technology portfolio that includes voice, security, wireless, and recently, storage networking for consumer, enterprise, and service provider markets. Cisco has managed to increase its manufacturing economies of scale and scope while growing its market presence and its leadership. To support its diverse product lines, Cisco has built a complex IT infrastructure consisting of numerous interconnected databases and applications, including a materials procurement electronic hub (e-hub). This e-hub serves real-time reporting and materials data for almost all of its contract manufacturers.

Each of these applications and databases connects into its mission-critical ERP and Cisco Connection Online (CCO) architectures responsible for online ordering, manufacturing, and financials databases. Almost every database has its own development and staging area and most production environments have standby sites for disaster recovery. The combination of these environments, including user home directories, currently consumes approximately 1.6 PB of raw storage.

Environment

Like many IT departments in the mid- to late-90s, the Cisco IT hosting group, whose infrastructure was aligned by business function, found itself supporting a vast array of applications of every imaginable size and criticality, from human resources and online sales tools to ERP financials and manufacturing databases.

By the beginning of 1999, it was clear that data storage was growing out of hand. In the fiscal years 2001 and 2002, data grew at 120 percent per year.[2] At the end of the 2002 fiscal year (July 2001), the depreciated, annualized TCO for IT storage was an estimated $0.010 per MB for 750 TB of raw storage. In 2003, that number dropped to $0.09 for approximately 1.2 PB of storage.

Of course these numbers, like most other storage inventory calculations at the time, were only estimates based on a weighted average of each type of storage hardware on site, which included a mix of different platforms from four different vendors.

Although industry pundits proclaimed that storage expenditures would decline as major ERP installations were postponed due to the market downturn, storage spending at Cisco remained constant and did not fall as a result of decreased infrastructure spending.[3]

A number of cross-functional and enterprise-wide IT initiatives helped to spur storage consumption at Cisco between 2000 and 2002. In particular, Cisco IT chose to proceed with its Oracle 11i implementation as part of its "breakaway strategy," which was designed to increase operational efficiencies and more closely integrate IT with business processes. At a time when most software and hardware consumers were scaling back expenditures and putting major initiatives on hold, Cisco launched its plan to migrate its Oracle 10.7 Financials and Manufacturing applications to Oracle 11i, an investment that required significant supplemental storage purchases, ranging between 50 TB and 500 TB.

Support Infrastructure

In 2000, Cisco formed a team of part-time storage and systems administrators to focus on storage allocation and de-allocation across enterprise hosting environments. 11 individuals spent between 20 and 100 percent of their time on day-to-day storage activities. Cisco steadily grew its storage purchase rate more than 100 percent per year and the average workload quickly became unmanageable. Strategic projects, such as creating standards policies and documenting best practices, took a back seat to tactical, operational duties, such as disk allocation and performance monitoring.

Concomitantly, Cisco formed a global virtual team of subject matter experts, with representation from engineering, networking, and datacenter infrastructure teams, to serve as a clearing house for storage-related information and to act as a steering committee for the adoption of internal storage standards. The Networked Storage Virtual Team (NSVT) served as a source of information and standards for early adoption of IP- and Fibre Channel-based storage networks and garnered much respect as a "one-stop shop" for accurate and up-to-date storage information.

Although the NSVT had wide-ranging success outside of IT hosting, it had little tangible success within IT hosting because of staff limitations and the size of the IT hosting storage environment, which continued to grow out of hand.

NOTE   The NSVT now incorporates all members of the IT hosting storage services team (now known as Enterprise Storage Services) and retains representation from several other cross-functional groups.

Within IT hosting, lowering TCO remained a priority. The absence of direct action toward that goal, however, resulted in little progress. To compensate, the storage services team created a storage vision initiative to provide guidelines for the future state of storage at Cisco. The vision was simple: Storage services would be provided either a la carte or as a utility with service-level provisions for varying degrees of availability and reliability to meet client requirements.

The need to streamline operations, reduce storage costs, and increase application availability drove the wholesale migration to SAN technology. To complete the storage vision initiative, however, appropriate technology enablers were required—specifically, a scalable, mission-critical, multi-service SAN switch and enterprise-ready software capable of managing hundreds of TB of storage. Achieving the storage vision would also require organizational measures, such as the creation of a dedicated storage management team to ensure that resources were properly aligned.

As Cisco entered the Fibre Channel market, software enablers were still lacking, but the hardware enablers seemed to be just over the horizon. Before outlining the current state of consolidated datacenter SANs at Cisco, it is important to note, however, that the roots of SAN implementations could be found in legacy environments dating back to 1998.

The Move to Storage Networks

In 1998, Cisco started to build its first Fibre Channel SANs. These prototype SANs were composed of fixed, 16-port switches that ran in arbitrated loop mode as part of Sequent NUMA clusters that hosted the mission-critical ERP environments. However, these switches were used almost exclusively as "dumb" hubs that simply provided additional port connectivity for large numbers of disks.

None of the functionality commonly associated with today's more sophisticated SAN technologies (Logical Unit Number [LUN] masking, Virtual SAN [VSAN], and Quality of Service [QoS]) was available.

As provisioning for multi-terabyte, direct-attached environments became more difficult, and as datacenter space constraints became increasingly taxed by high storage and server growth rates, technical subject matter experts (internal Cisco resources) considered moving both production data processing and backups onto SANs. However, because of the specific requirements of each application and the decentralized nature of the storage management teams, discrete SAN islands began to emerge across the company.

At that time, each virtual storage administrator represented a business vertical and was responsible for different applications with different requirements. Each environment had heterogeneous DAS configured according to different standards. Correspondingly, as one can imagine, each SAN island was created differently. Many storage arrays were older frames with SCSI adapters that required upgrades to Fibre Channel disk adapters before they could be attached to a SAN. Likewise, most hosts had SCSI host bus adapters (HBAs) and required upgrades to Fibre Channel.

These early SANs presented storage administrators with severe challenges. HBA interoperability was one. Because Cisco had already purchased a large number of disparate HBAs with proprietary software drivers, many hosts were unable to move directly to a SAN without multiple outages to install and configure HBAs. In some instances, HBA drivers had to be upgraded multiple times to successfully attach to SAN storage.

Another obstacle to the storage vision was the lack of a scalable SAN switch capable of supporting the largest Cisco applications. For example, to build a consolidated SAN to support ERP using the largest switches on the market at that time would have required the deployment of 10 64-port, director-class switches interconnected using inter-switch links (ISLs). Dedicating switch ports to connect one switch to another (rather than a server or a storage device) increased management complexities while decreasing operational efficiencies.

In summary, as the Cisco storage administrators continued to build more SAN islands, which restricted the sharing of storage across business verticals, increases in utilization rates plateaued.

Implementation

While continuing to search for the technology enablers to support the storage vision, Cisco reorganized the storage support team to better align with the vision's goals. The first move was to trim the operational team from 11 part-time storage administrators to six full-time storage administrators (and three full-time project managers) led by Scott Zimmer, senior IT manager, and Brian Christensen, director of IT business systems hosting. As the new team, named Enterprise Storage Services (ESS), became a cohesive unit, its focus shifted from ad-hoc firefighting to a more strategic direction of enabling standards and repeatable installations. Accordingly, the new storage team was tasked with critical business-impacting initiatives, such as consolidation of DAS and SAN islands to an enterprise-wide SAN infrastructure.

At the same time, Cisco started its negotiations to purchase Andiamo Systems, a startup venture that was building the next-generation Fibre Channel director, in which Cisco was the sole outside investor.

The Cisco SAN islands were comprised of a mix of fixed Brocade and McDATA Fibre Channel switches, which had grown to over 100 in number. As the impending release of the first generation MDS 9000 switches from Cisco/Andiamo approached, however, the team halted additional SAN switch purchases long enough to certify the MDS 9000 switches for use in its own datacenter. This certification process entailed participation in a lengthy beta process as well as interoperability and performance testing with numerous products from various disk, software, and HBA vendors.

The Enterprise Storage Services team wasted no time implementing the new solution. The first deployment of the MDS 9509 switches in the Cisco datacenters came directly on the heels of completing the MDS 9000 beta program. As soon as the MDS hardware was released, it was deployed in the Cisco development and disaster recovery datacenters in Research Triangle Park (RTP), North Carolina.

NOTE   The Cisco IT department has a management objective to be the "first and best" Cisco customer, whereby Cisco IT provides product feedback early and often during each phase of the development and deployment life cycles. In addition, the Cisco-on-Cisco initiative dictates that wherever possible, Cisco run its IT operations on Cisco products. It is important to note, however, that the MDS platform was chosen, not mandated, as a technology enabler for the storage vision, based solely on its performance and its high availability (HA) capabilities.

In January of 2003, four MDS 9509s were deployed directly into the ERP and data warehousing development and disaster recovery environments in RTP, NC. In this environment, 11 HP-UX hosts and approximately 100 TB of storage were split across two SAN islands. The first SAN island, composed of seven HP hosts and 11 EMC Symmetrix frames, was built on a core of four McDATA, 32-port switches, two on each path, connected via ISLs. The second SAN island with the remaining four hosts was built on a core of two 32-port McDATAs attached to one Hewlett-Packard XP XP512 storage array. This environment is shown in Figure 8-1.

The cutover from the legacy McDATA environment to the MDS 9000 was done in two stages. In the first stage, one path in each SAN island was patched through one Cisco MDS 9509 director. Each director was configured with four 16-port Fibre Channel line cards and three 32-port Fibre Channel line cards to allow for maximum bandwidth to multiple environments in the future. The first stage of the cutover is shown in Figure 8-2.

Figure 8-1   *Legacy Cisco SAN Islands*

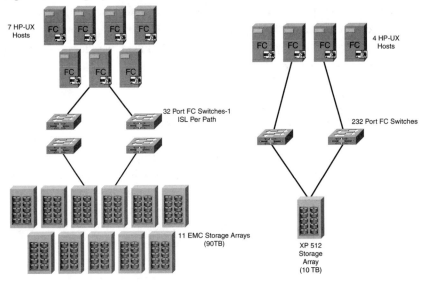

Figure 8-2   *Legacy SAN Migration—Stage 1*

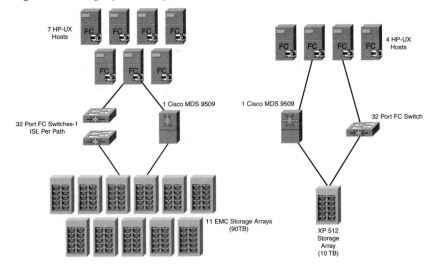

Because the MDS 9000 was still a relatively new product, the team decided to run the applications dual-pathed through both the MDS 9000 and the McDATA switches for four weeks. This was long enough to demonstrate assured stability and performance, particularly for the ERP application, long considered one of the "crown jewels" of IT.

After four weeks with no issues, the second and final stage of the migration was completed when the team removed the connections to the McDATA switches and collapsed both SAN islands into one MDS fabric with four MDS 9509s (connected with two four-port ISLs).

Each cutover was completed during business hours with no disruption in service to the applications in question, one of which was a heavily utilized manufacturing development environment accessed by developers around the clock.

The final stage of the migration is shown in Figure 8-3.

Figure 8-3 *Legacy SAN Migration—Stage 2*

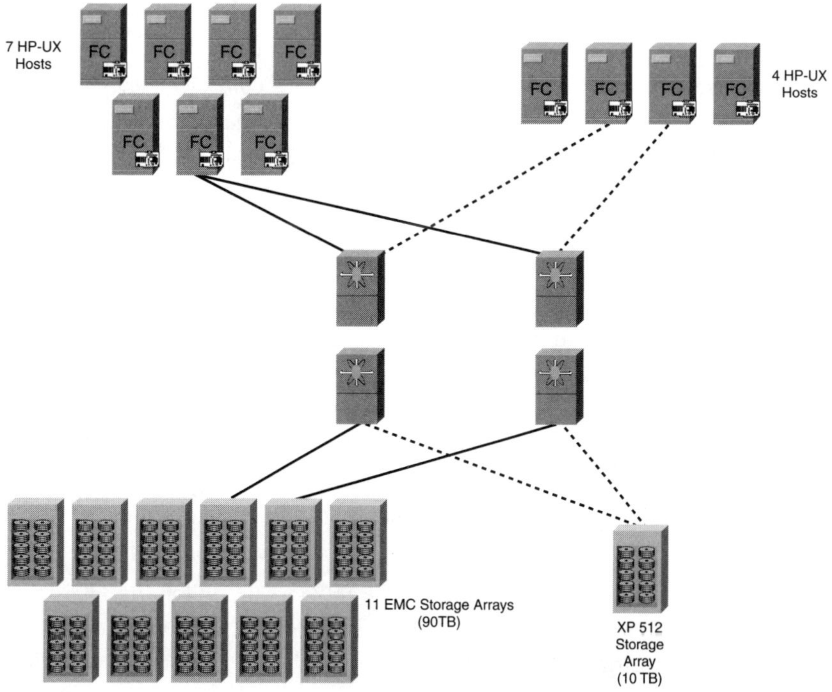

To build a similar fabric that provided the capacity, performance, and reliability required to support the ever-growing ERP environment, the team would have needed to deploy a minimum of ten McDATA directors and dedicate many of those ports to ISLs. In short, the team would have needed to purchase two and a half times more McDATA switches to simulate the fabric built with the four MDS 9509s.

In addition to being scalable, the Enterprise Storage Services team found the Cisco MDS solution to be easy to manage and monitor with Cisco Fabric Manager, an integrated set of software tools that allows management and real-time monitoring of the Cisco MDS 9000 Family devices.

In addition to providing highly-available and robust SAN connectivity for the foundation of the storage utility vision, the MDS platform was also leveraged as part of an overall plan to lower operational expenditures and to reduce the total points of management. In the third and fourth quarter of 2003, multiple MDS units were aggressively deployed as the backbone of a major storage consolidation project.

Since the first migration, all SAN islands based on McDATA and Brocade switches have been replaced with MDS switches in Cisco datacenters around the world. In total, 142 Brocade and McDATA fixed switches and two McDATA directors were replaced with only 32 director-class MDS platform switches.

Long-term plans for SAN connectivity include collapsing all independent SAN fabrics into a single consolidated SAN infrastructure per datacenter, and linking all campus datacenters in each location over intercampus dark fiber with Fibre Channel over IP (FCIP). In addition, a major rollout of iSCSI is planned for 2005 and 2006.

Consolidation

Storage growth at Cisco remained unchecked across business units in IT from the latter part of the 1990s until early 2003. Given the disparate nature of the storage management initiatives and of the groups managing the storage, a significant number of purchases continued to be made, even though allocation efficiency hovered around 20 to 30 percent.

As the Enterprise Storage Services team began to gain traction and to share best practices, management determined that a significant cost savings could be achieved with a major consolidation effort. Management determined that, in addition to saving on maintenance bills and deferring datacenter expansions, a consolidation effort could increase economies of scale by reducing the number of points of management.

After negotiations with its primary storage vendor, Cisco agreed to purchase eight external RAID arrays in January, 2003 to consolidate 80 older frames, which were fully depreciated but carried a maintenance expense of over 4 millions dollars per year. The additional depreciation expense of the eight new frames was offset by immediate relief of the budgeted maintenance expense for the first year (and additional subsequent years for the life of the hardware). Although the project itself was monumental—crossing multiple business units and involving over 30 outages to install FC HBAs into hosts which were previously DAS SCSI—it was completed at budget and only two months behind schedule.

Initially, significant delays faced the project team stemming from two datacenter-related issues. The first was that the RTP datacenter was found to be at its maximum weight capacity in some locations. One month previous to the arrival of the consolidation hardware, management formed a "tiger team" that was dedicated to moving storage frames that were not on the consolidation list to make room for the new hardware.

The second issue causing delays in the project was the decision to deploy structured fiber cabling as part of the overall SAN infrastructure. Structured fiber offers significant management advantages over ad-hoc runs of fiber under the datacenter floor. When a structured fiber installation is completed, all fiber drops are patched through centralized patch panels and additional SAN storage capacity can be added without installing additional fiber.

The deployment of structured cabling even without the consolidation project would have been a significant undertaking. The two projects combined required monumental effort on the part of the storage and datacenter staff. After the structured cabling design was approved, and the cabling had begun, the new environment began to take shape. The consolidation hardware was deployed, and system administrators started copying host environments to the new locations. Unfortunately, a large number of the new fiber connectors were faulty and had to be replaced. During this time, the host environments could not be copied and the consolidation project was temporarily put on hold.

Approximately one month after the project had officially begun and all faulty connectors had been replaced, the migrations were allowed to proceed. Between February and August, 2003, almost 100 hosts were migrated to new storage and to new Cisco MDS switches. In addition to lowering the TCO and showcasing the new Cisco SAN solutions, the consolidated environments provided an additional buffer for storage growth. Because the new disks had been reorganized and restriped, the database environments also displayed better utilization and better performance.

An unexpected consequence of the consolidation project was that numerous other host and database candidates for decommissioning and consolidation were discovered. As part of the process of turning off ports on disk frames and running cable traces, several "forgotten" systems were unearthed and the removal of them offered additional opportunities to lower the cost of storage and host maintenance. As a result of the first storage consolidation effort, a host consolidation project was initiated in tandem with the evaluation of several platforms for wide-scale Linux farm deployments.

TCO and ROI

The first attempt to document storage TCO at Cisco began in October, 2002. A number of different home grown tools were used to tally the number, type, and capacity of frames, network-attached storage (NAS) devices, SAN switches, and other capital expenditures related to storage. Subsequently, estimates were made for acquisition costs for each type of device. A weighted average of all frame types across the enterprise was then multiplied by the different cost structures for each device to come up with a total cost per MB across the enterprise. Additional data related to labor was compiled and then added to the overall per MB costs. The results from the study concluded that storage cost structures were in line with overall industry averages at approximately $0.10 per MB.

Although the study produced reasonably accurate estimates of storage-related costs in IT, the study also revealed that Cisco was still in need of an automated resource reporting infrastructure. During this period of time, the SRM solution Cisco had chosen was just being rolled out and lacked the capability to supply meaningful data.

Based on the estimated cost per MB, as documented in the TCO study, the savings associated with migrating one MB from DAS to SAN storage approached $0.01 per MB, per year. Estimates of overall savings for a single migration of a 150-TB DAS environment to SAN storage reached as high as $1,500,000–$7,500,000 for an additional 750 TB.

The Net Present Value (NPV) for the first phase of consolidation was positive and the project was positioned to create significant value based purely on the maintenance waiver, although with the additional migration of DAS to SAN storage, the ROI would surpass 50 percent.

Over the long-term, the increase in depreciation expenses associated with the additional hardware was offset by the relief from millions of dollars in maintenance fees for the frames to be consolidated. With the completion of the project, datacenters that were already at capacity found much needed relief with the removal of 80 storage frames. Consequently, a planned datacenter expansion was put on hold, offering a significant cost-avoidance opportunity.

The decision to deploy the MDS platform switches in conjunction with the consolidation effort led to a sizable shift in the amount of storage migrated from DAS to SAN. Early estimates projected that before the first round of consolidation, approximately 70 to 80 percent of all non-NAS storage was direct-attached, and only 20 to 30 percent was SAN-attached (spread across numerous SAN islands). Post-consolidation numbers indicated that at least 50 percent of all storage at Cisco had been migrated to a SAN architecture by the end of the first consolidation phase, decreasing the estimates for the amount of time required to complete the execution of the storage vision.

NOTE	Although exact numbers are still hard to come by, some "back-of-the-envelope" math indicates that at a TCO difference of $0.01 per MB between DAS and SAN storage, the direct savings from the first consolidation project (and from moving from 30 percent SAN storage to 50 percent SAN storage) approached $1,500,000. (150 TB×1000 GB per TB×1000 MB per GB×$0.01 per MB).

A second round of consolidation was planned for the 2004 fiscal year, and it had a similarly wide-ranging impact in terms of both space and cost savings. Ongoing consolidation of both storage and servers in the enterprise is a high-visibility initiative for Cisco IT as they analyze the requirements for migrating to a grid-computing model based on Linux farms and networked storage.

NOTE	An updated TCO study in May, 2004 indicated that the consolidation of environments on to the MDS platform decreased the TCO by an additional 20 percent.

Tiered Storage Implementation

The Enterprise Storage Services team is also in the process of gathering requirements for a tiered storage infrastructure that is capable of supporting an Information Lifecycle Management (ILM) program to lower costs and help advance the storage vision.

Although utilizing homogeneous storage currently offers significant economies of scale and decreased management costs, over time the ability to support and scale a multiplatform, multi-vendor storage environment offers greater increases in savings and operational efficiencies. To accomplish this goal, a tiered-storage infrastructure is required.

A technology assessment is in process for the 2005 fiscal year to determine the feasibility and impact of implementing mid-range storage for applications with less stringent performance and availability requirements. Until the management interfaces and software required for migrating the data from the high-end to the mid-range storage are more mature, however, wholesale migration plans will be subject to scrutiny. Initial engagements are expected to be done on a smaller scale for isolated environments. The ability to track the total amounts and costs of storage at each tier, and the ability to estimate the useful life of the data in question, is not currently feasible; however, as software to manage data migrations becomes fully mature, tiered storage solutions will be implemented as quickly as possible.

Capacity Planning and Utilization

During the boom times, it is safe to say that little was done in the way of capacity planning. With triple-digit growth rates in 1999 and 2000, the sole objective was to provide basic storage support for environments before the applications (and the business units depending on them) came to a halt.

In more recent history, the process of yearly and quarterly capacity planning for storage purchases took many hours of research and measurement for each environment. Purchases were closely examined and justified as part of either growth or a specific project or initiative. Historical trends were analyzed in an attempt to project growth rates for each quarter of the fiscal year, and although it was a labor-intensive process, it generally yielded fairly accurate data for planning purposes.

Today, storage capacity planning is typically handled as part of the ongoing consolidation strategy. All purchases are closely scrutinized; however, buffers included in the annual consolidation purchase typically carry most of the business verticals for several months after the initial consolidation. One exception to this rule is the Oracle 11i development environment, which tends to grow from 30 percent to 100 percent annually. Capacity planning for this environment is handled separately and purchases are made on a case-by-case basis apart from the quarterly planning cycles.

In 2001, allocation efficiency was estimated to be between 20 percent and 30 percent with no estimates for utilization efficiencies. Growth was manually tracked for most environments, but the inability to share storage between groups created a stove-piped environment, thereby hampering any concerted attempts to increase utilization rates.

In 2002, storage allocation efficiency reached the 40 percent range with the creation of larger SAN islands and the decommissioning of more DAS environments. Allocation efficiency since the MDS deployment is now in the 50-60 percent range and another project in the coming year will migrate the remaining DAS environments to SANs.

Storage Recovery

In late 2003 and early 2004, estimates for overall allocation efficiency approached 60 percent. Remaining DAS devices are increasingly consolidated into collapsed-core SAN fabrics built on MDS 9509s, boosting allocation efficiency rates. Data collected by the Storage Recovery Program—a cross-functional program designed to address the demand side of the storage equation by reducing the number of purchases required by application groups—indicates that allocation efficiency might also be as high as 70 percent.

NOTE   Note that in some companies, storage recovery efforts are referred to as *storage mining*.

Raising the utilization efficiency rate is one of the main objectives of the Storage Recovery Program at Cisco. Piyush Bhargava, manager of the Enterprise Data Integrity team, has initiated a novel approach to the problem of storage reclamation by creating the Bytes Back Club, a rewards-based system whereby system administrators, database administrators, and project managers are eligible to receive financial rewards for releasing storage to be reused by other groups. In its first year, the SRP team, in conjunction with the Bytes Back Club, reclaimed an estimated $2.9 million dollars of unused storage.

As of February, 2004, Cisco had migrated off of Brocade and McDATA Fibre Channel switches and on to MDS-based SANs. Additional long-term goals include the migration of SANs in each datacenter into a consolidated SAN infrastructure (with separate virtual SANs [VSANs] for logical management of disks assigned to different business verticals), and the migration of all remaining DAS to either Fibre Channel or iSCSI SANs.

Cost and management savings, as well as performance increases, will be sought as part of a rollout of Linux blade farms for high availability and low-cost compute services. The concept of virtualization applies here insofar as increasing the utilization of the server resource, the CPU, lowers the TCO for the server, just as increasing disk utilization lowers the TCO for the disk.

In addition to multiple storage consolidation efforts, the storage team intends to migrate away from modem-based, dial-up access for remote monitoring of storage frames to an IP-based model that utilizes VPN access methods. The Enterprise Storage Services team will drive other projects, which include deploying iSCSI and virtualization products, outlining a template for end-to-end architecture, instituting a service-level management framework for storage services, and selecting a solution for long-distance replication.

In addition, the Enterprise Storage Services team is in the process of deploying an SATA solution to lower the TCO of one the largest single environments at Cisco, a multi-terabyte repository for code binaries.

Conclusion

The rapid pace at which Cisco IT has deployed the Cisco MDS 9000 Series Multilayer switch indicates a shift in priorities from cautious investigation of new technologies to a willingness to accept an incremental level of risk to more quickly achieve the vision set out almost three years ago. Business continuance and disaster recovery strategies continue to receive significant focus, and the adoption of newer technologies helps add functionality and further stratify the tiers that are supported by Enterprise Storage Services.

Although the ability to support greater numbers of terabytes of storage at Cisco currently hinges on the homogeneous nature of its storage install base, as storage software management products mature, Cisco expects the costs of managing heterogeneous storage to decrease over time.

References

[1]Cisco Systems, Inc. (2003). Form 10-K for the Fiscal Year Ended July 26, 2003. Annual Report. Retrieved June 3, 2004 from EDGAR.

[2]Williams, Bill. "IT Storage Total Cost of Ownership—Internal White Paper," Cisco Systems, Inc., 2002: page 3.

[3]Ibid.

CHAPTER 9

RETAIL
GROCER

NOTE   At Storage Networking World in Phoenix, Arizona in April, 2004, I met and spoke with a 14-year IT veteran who is the director of technical services at a major U.S. retail grocer. He participated in a Cisco-sponsored customer event where we discussed consolidation initiatives and his company's decision to deploy the Cisco MDS Multilayer Director switch. His experiences are the basis for this chapter.

Although this case study is anonymously presented, concrete financial figures regarding TCO have been omitted at the request of the parties involved. Because the storage network infrastructure outlined in this case study is still in its infancy, concrete financial figures regarding cost savings and cost avoidances are forthcoming. Although financial analysis is a key component of any case study, the reader is encouraged to find value in the presentation of items that highlight other key components from Part 1, "The Storage Networking Value Proposition," namely, the consolidation of SAN islands to large datacenter SANs to increase utilization and operational efficiencies.

As noted previously, operational efficiencies related to flexibility and ease of management are difficult to quantify outside of the terabytes (TB) per administrator metric, which includes measurable components, such as the number, frequency, and duration of storage-related activities.

A critical function of the storage decision maker is to understand the principle contribution of new technologies and to make informed decisions regarding his own infrastructure, even when the long-term benefits of storage networking are not easily quantified. Although Net Present Value (NPV) and Return On Investment (ROI) analysis is fundamental to the decision-making process, the current lack of readily available tools for measuring utilization and operational efficiencies impairs visibility of the immediate impact of deploying new storage solutions.

Between the deployment and the evaluation phases of storage networking rollouts, when visibility is typically at its poorest, it is crucial to maintain adherence to the storage vision and to trust that operational efficiencies, though difficult to measure, are quickly realized after the learning curve is achieved. These efficiencies are typically significant enough to justify in the short-term storage networking projects that enable the storage vision until successful, quantifiable results can be achieved.

This case study highlights the fact that the early adoption of new technologies can be tied directly to a strategy for long-term growth and customer care. Although concrete numbers regarding allocation efficiency and utilization efficiency are difficult to pinpoint, the financial value of the solution documented here are, over time, measured primarily in terms of operational efficiency and increased availability.

The migration to the Cisco MDS platform illustrates this company's belief in a storage vision built on the following principles:

- Multiple storage transport protocols

- Virtualized disk subsystems

- Centralized storage management

Executive Summary

This firm is recognized by many as one of the leading retail grocers in terms of technology adoption and deployment. With over 200 stores in the United States and more than $4 billion in sales in 2003, this firm shows that it is possible to grow without jeopardizing the quality, service, and customer focus for which it is famous. For many years, this firm has consistently demonstrated a strategy for growth that includes the early adoption of many innovations in the food marketing and retailing industry, without sacrificing a commitment to customer care and community well-being.

In the early 1990s, Efficient Consumer Response (ECR) began as a formal initiative in the United States, similar to a previous effort known as Quick Response (QR). Both of these programs were designed to shrink the order inventory cycle for grocery retailers and to shorten the time between realizing the need for additional product and having it restocked and on the shelves.[1]

In short, ECR is a broader effort to bolster and streamline grocery supply chains, specifically in the United States, although efforts similar to ECR have appeared in Europe, Canada, Australia, and parts of South America.[2]

The process of innovation adoption, as discussed in Chapter 4, "How it Should Be Done: Implementation Strategies and Best Practices", is much like the process of technology adoption, in that a select few companies (early adopters) are quick to implement new products or ideas that offer the promise of a competitive edge, whereas other companies (mainstream adopters and laggards) let early adopters lead the charge, so that they can learn from their competitors' successes or mistakes.

In addition to adopting many ECR-related innovations such as Continuous Replenishment Programs (CRPs), this firm has consistently led its competitors in the deployment of innovative IT solutions, helping it gain a competitive edge in retailing.

NOTE   CRP uses Computer Assisted Ordering (CAO) technologies to simplify the process of inventory management.[3]

This firm was one of the first grocers to adopt barcode scanning technology, and has aggressively deployed electronic shelf labels (ESLs), which allow retailers to simultaneously update prices in multiple locations from a single application. ESL technology enables the company to spend more time serving the customer and less time marking prices.

Just as this firm's leading-edge adoption of new business processes has helped it gain and preserve sizable market share, its adoption of storage networking technologies supports a strategic framework for lowering costs, streamlining operations, and increasing efficiencies.

Storage Environment

The evolution of storage networking deployments at this firm followed a familiar trajectory (from direct-attached storage [DAS] to small SAN islands, and finally, to consolidated SANs) in the support of implementing storage as a networked, utility-like service. To understand the components of this company's storage vision, it is beneficial to take a closer look at the firm's IT infrastructure and how IT plays a critical role in the overall business strategy.

With 60 TB of usable storage spread across three datacenters (one production site, one disaster recovery site, and one development site), the IT leadership at this firm has spent considerable time and energy analyzing methods for increasing storage management efficiencies while simultaneously supporting a varying array of highly advanced application technologies. The company currently supports a two-tiered, client-server architecture comprised of a number of home-grown and off-the-shelf applications that reside on approximately 160 Windows servers, and a number of corporate back-office applications distributed across approximately 20 enterprise class UNIX and Linux servers.

Each of the company's more than 200 stores sends business-critical pricing and payroll data back to corporate headquarters over a frame-relay/Asynchronous Transfer Mode (ATM) connection. An in-house CAO application designed to streamline inventory operations for perishables and groceries resides at each location and sends daily updates back to headquarters. The data is then analyzed at headquarters and the orders are passed on to vendors and distributors for fulfillment.

By design, the CAO application is capable of forecasting up to three days' worth of orders, with the caveat that the accuracy of the projection decreases as the length of the forecast increases. The capacity to project up to three days of orders in advance allows inventory to be shipped, even in the event of a catastrophic loss of service at either of the main sites. This is one of the most advanced CAO implementations in the industry; many grocers still rely on manual intervention for determining when inventory levels are low and for reordering products.

Just as CAO data is pushed from each store to headquarters, updated pricing information is distributed from corporate headquarters to each store over the same frame-relay/ATM network. Where applicable, any changes in prices are sent in real-time to the ESLs, where liquid crystal display (LCD) monitors under each item display the most current prices for that item.

To support these advanced technologies, a similarly advanced hardware infrastructure (technology enabler) was required. Based on initial analyses showing the potential for increased economies of scale, increased operational efficiency, and reductions in hardware maintenance stemming from consolidating storage platforms, the management team determined that deploying storage networks was the appropriate solution.

Today the ratio of DAS-to-SAN storage stands at approximately 70 percent SAN (42 TB usable) with a high visibility project slated to migrate the remaining UNIX DAS to networked storage as soon as possible.

The Move to Storage Networks

The initial evaluation and deployment of SAN technology began in 2001 as point solutions for environments that the director of technical services and his team determined had inordinately low disk utilization rates.

Early evaluations of SAN technology made the team hopeful for the benefits of increased utilization and availability; however, the team was skeptical of the technology's capability to deliver on its promises. Initial cost-benefit analyses showed the potential for an early uptick in support costs and management inefficiencies after accounting for a steep learning curve and the interoperability issues endemic in what was then a relatively immature industry. Although initial pre-deployment data supported fears of higher costs, the team was not deterred from deploying SANs, although they did adopt a "wait-and-see" attitude as the first rollouts were completed.

The first storage network to be deployed was a dual-fabric SAN built on two 32-port fixed Brocade Fibre Channel (FC) switches, supporting a backup environment. This SAN was designed to move backup traffic off of the IP backbone and onto the FC network, thereby lessening the impact on the IP network and increasing backup performance.

Four more SAN islands were deployed between 2001 and 2003, but as these SAN islands became more prevalent, one fact became glaringly obvious:

Supporting a number of SAN islands was only marginally more efficient than supporting several individual DAS environments. In fact, SAN islands were really only direct-connect environments that utilized FC switches as dumb hubs for increased connectivity. Inter-Switch Links (ISLs) were not used to consolidate environments or to share capacity, and ultimately many ports on FC switches remained unused, indicating a relapse into higher costs and poor utilization.

SAN Consolidation

As part of the firm's storage vision and in keeping with the corporate philosophy of streamlined and consolidated operations, in 2003, the team decided to tighten up the storage infrastructure by moving the SAN islands to consolidated datacenter SANs.

The team chose the Cisco Systems MDS 9509 Multilayer Director for the consolidated SAN architecture. The team replaced the SAN islands with two dual-fabric SANs per production datacenter, each built on two MDS 9509s. A fifth MDS 9509 resides in the development datacenter and is used for testing firmware upgrades and for simulating changes to virtual SANs (VSANs) in production. Through the use of VSANs, the team can simulate all production environments on the one development switch.

In addition to VSAN technology, one of the key factors behind choosing the Cisco solution is the support it provides for multiple platforms in one box. The team already uses Fibre Channel over IP (FCIP) over a T3 connection for database archive log shipment between the primary and secondary datacenters, and believes that the widespread use of iSCSI for additional SAN extensions is not far off. With the price of FC HBAs decreasing, however, the team feels that the urgent need to deploy iSCSI has diminished somewhat. Having the ability to utilize multiple transport protocols in the same chassis offers significant investment protection, regardless of the final decision.

Although the initial costs of investing in SAN technology were higher— particularly in terms of the learning curve for the support staff—the team contends that over time the strategy has proven sound. Subsequent increases in management efficiencies have made up for the costs associated with deploying the new technology. Because the deployment of storage networks at this firm is still relatively young, hard numbers indicating the exact scale of the improvements are still forthcoming. Some immediate benefits of storage networking are readily apparent, however:

- The process of storage provisioning has been simplified.

- Utilization rates, as expected, have increased.

- Management costs related to storage support have decreased.

Currently, the technology support team does not have dedicated storage managers. To support 60 TB of storage, two UNIX systems administrators act as virtual storage managers and spend approximately 40 percent of their time on storage. The leadership team is in the process of centralizing the management of storage, which might lead to the creation of a dedicated storage team. The team cautions, however, that the operational efficiencies gained through the use of storage networks decreases the need for a large team of people focused solely on storage.

Future Initiatives

Going forward, the team explains that they will concentrate on fulfilling the vision of enterprise networked storage offered as a utility for their clients. Integral to the success of the storage vision is the upgrade of the IP network backbone and the ongoing evaluation of both hardware and software replication technologies to augment business continuance capabilities.

As mentioned earlier, with the addition of the IP Storage Services Modules to the Cisco MDS 9509 multi-service switches, the team has already begun to use FCIP between the primary and secondary datacenters. The long-term goal is to replicate the critical production data to the disaster recovery site as quickly as possible to minimize the amount of time that production data is available only at the primary site. To that end, the team states that they want to implement a disk-staging strategy utilizing FCIP between the two locations.

Because prices for fiber remain competitive, the team is willing to look at adding more fiber between the primary and secondary sites; however, the team believes eventually it will choose to implement either Course Wave Division Multiplexing (CWDM) or Dense Wave Division Multiplexing (DWDM) (or a hybrid of the two technologies) to optimize the bandwidth between the production and disaster recovery sites. In the interim, the team plans to continue using FCIP over the IP backbone.

The continued migration of UNIX applications to the Linux platform is another highly visible project, as is further testing of iSCSI on the IP Storage Services Module, and the deployment of blade servers directly onto the SAN configured to boot over Fibre Channel. The team has also evaluated networked-attached storage but currently sees no need for NAS in the environment.

Conclusion

The firm sees storage networks as a fundamental technology enabler for virtualization, which will enable the "holy grail," the capability to move data between locations and across storage platforms transparent to the applications and hosts. This capability, in addition to raising utilization rates, will also enhance the overall business continuance strategy.

Although the team recognizes that ease of management for heterogeneous storage is still a myth, and that software capable of supporting an advanced ILM infrastructure is still to come, the team sees value in a tiered storage infrastructure. The team also recognizes that the first step toward achieving the "holy grail," and ultimately fulfilling the storage vision is migrating all DAS to a storage network.

References

[1]Food Marking Institute. "FMI Media Backgrounder— Efficient Consumer Response," http://www.fmi.org/media/bg/ecr1.htm, 2004.

[2]Ibid.

[3]Ibid.

CHAPTER 10

FINANCIAL SERVICES

NOTE   In April and May, 2004, I spoke at length with a team of representatives from a major European financial services firm. The team discussed with me the challenges they face supporting multiple, high availability SAN fabrics across three time zones. Their experiences form the basis for this chapter.

Although this case study is presented as anonymous, concrete financial figures regarding total cost of ownership (TCO) are omitted at the request of the parties involved. Concrete financial figures regarding cost savings and cost avoidances are also omitted from this discussion. Although financial analysis is a key component of any case study, you are encouraged to find value in the presentation of items that highlight other key components from Part 1, "The Storage Networking Value Proposition," namely, the use of SAN extensions to increase the availability and reliability of the storage infrastructure.

As noted previously, operational efficiencies related to flexibility and ease of management are difficult to quantify outside the terabytes (TB) per administrator metric, which includes measurable components, such as the number, frequency, and duration of storage-related activities.

Executive Summary

This firm is one of the world's leading exchanges for money market and derivatives trading, supporting billions of dollars worth of trades per day.

This firm began in the early 1980s as a commodities and futures exchange that was specifically designed to offer institutions access to investments in foreign markets. This firm now offers customers a broad portfolio of derivatives products including short term interest rates (STIRs), bonds, swaps, equities, and commodities.

To understand the value of the services provided by this firm and to understand the volume of transactions this firm processes, it is helpful to understand how derivatives work. Although the discussion of derivatives might seem indulgent, I believe the concept of balancing exposure, risks, and rewards is analogous to the concept of early adoption and innovation, specifically with regard to implementing new technology.

Derivatives—specifically options, swaps, and futures—are financial instruments used by private individuals and institutions to create wealth and to balance portfolios. At minimum, a derivative can be described as an investment whose worth is tied to the valuation of a wholly separate and distinct financial instrument.

Derivatives allow individuals who desire increased levels of risk, or alternately, reduced exposure to risk, to hedge against fluctuations in broader markets and to protect (and ostensibly to increase) revenue streams associated with their investments.

How Derivatives Work

Here follows a brief discussion of how derivatives can be used to minimize risk and protect income. Because the value of the derivative is abstracted from the value of the underlying asset, it is possible to construct complex financial management strategies and to build portfolios comprised of investments in both the principle asset and a set of derivative assets whose values can rise or fall in opposition to each other. Three of the most common examples of derivatives are options, swaps, and futures.

Options tend to work in the following manner: Investors might hold an equity position as a long-term investment with the understanding that the value of the asset might decline over time. To recognize revenue from the asset, the owner must liquidate his position in the asset. An option is a contract that offers the right to purchase or sell a position in a particular asset at a fixed price by a certain date in time. The purchase of an option does not require ownership of the underlying asset. An option to sell (put) or an option to buy (call) retains value until the time of its expiration. Ownership of an option can significantly minimize the risk involved with a long-term equity position.

In a similar manner, corporations and financial institutions often use swaps and futures to minimize the risk inherent in holding large positions in volatile currencies and commodities.

Currency swaps are typically used by corporations with a significant business presence in a foreign country to dampen the impact of currency rate fluctuations.

Futures differ from options in that they are a binding contract to purchase a set amount of a commodity at an agreed-upon price at some time in the future. Options are the right (not the obligation) to execute a buy or sell contract for a particular asset.

After derivative trades are executed, they are then handled by a settlement firm or a clearing house that processes daily margin calls. Because derivatives do not require ownership in the underlying asset, it is often said that derivatives traders trade purely in risk.

One other note of consequence: Because of the phenomenon known as purchasing power parity or the Law of One Price, which dictates that in open or global markets there can be no arbitrage, prices of derivatives and the value of their underlying assets tend to converge as contract dates reach expiration. Accordingly, the level of risk associated with the derivative tends to dissipate over time.

Derivatives, despite being esoteric and complicated financial tools used to build significant sums of wealth (think alchemy), are a fundamental, integral piece of global financial markets and their use is widespread among private and institutional investors alike.

Storage Environment

This firm's primary datacenter is hosted in London; secondary datacenters in Chicago and Paris also provide additional capacity and resiliency.

The primary datacenter and the Paris datacenter are connected to each other over a pair of Synchronous Digital Hierarchy (SDH) rings (the European equivalent of a Synchronous Optical Network [SONET] ring). These links are completely independent of each other and share no common infrastructure. Chicago attaches to the optical ring via an IP Point of Presence (POP) in London.

The IT operations group currently supports 60 TB of raw storage across all three locations; the application data is replicated to each datacenter as dictated by business need.

Approximately 20 TB of that 60 TB is for core applications hosted on Virtual Memory System (VMS) platform servers from Digital Equipment Corporation connected to a Brocade SAN infrastructure. The remaining 40 TB of raw storage is split between the main datacenter, Chicago, and Paris and resides on a mix of high-end and mid-tier storage arrays from Hitachi Data Systems™. 10 Cisco MDS 9509 multilayer director switches form the core SAN infrastructure.

The Cisco MDS 9509s are configured with a combination of 16- and 32-port line cards to take advantage of both the line-rate performance of the 16-port cards and the price performance of the 32-port cards. In general, the 32-port cards are used primarily for development and test environments (which require less maximum throughput at peak performance times), whereas the 16-port cards are used for storage and connectivity for production hosts.

NOTE   This configuration takes advantage of the 3.38 to 1 oversubscription rate of the 32-port cards on the MDS platform.

Each application environment is typically configured for three times the maximum required performance. Although an average day might see 3.6 million trades, the firm must provide headroom for sustained performance of over ten million trades. It is critical for the firm to process all trades in a single day so that trades can be cleared through a clearing house, such as ClearNet, in time to make daily margin calls. In no way can the firm afford to get behind in its transaction processing; the downstream effects of a backlog of trades could be economically disastrous.

Each trade goes through a series of gates from bid to completion as part of its life cycle. The trade registration system (TRS) receives trades through trading desktops and application front-ends. From there, the relevant data for each trade (contract specifications, expiration dates, and so on) is passed to the primary database where the trade data is then logged and stored. When the trade is executed, the trade data is sent back to the TRS. From the TRS, it is sent to the clearing house for reconciliation of margin calls. As the final step of each trade's life cycle, data from the clearing house regarding the client'ss financial standing and risk exposure is then posted back into the primary database.

This type of environment (multiple-staging environments for data transfer between numerous applications) is common to many financial institutions, as is the reliance upon storage networking technologies to provide increased availability and reliability.

The Move to Storage Networks

The decision to implement SAN storage at this firm was based on the need for cost efficiency and additional functionality for application environments. To support a major migration effort from VAX to Alpha in 2001, the storage support staff realized new technology was required.

The firm became an early adopter of SAN technology almost three years ago with its initial implementation of Fibre Channel (FC) switches to support shared, clustered file systems for their VAX-to-Alpha migration. This first SAN environment was built to allow booting directly off of the SAN fabric (with no local host storage required), and it eventually grew to 20 fixed Brocade switches. A year later, the support team began moving Windows and Solaris systems to Fibre Channel SANs attached to high-end external storage arrays from Hitachi Data Systems™.

Over time, the proliferation of SAN islands and the manageability of multiple SANs across several discrete datacenters became a source of inefficiency. To reduce the number of SANs in the environment, the team began consolidating SAN islands onto the Cisco MDS platform. In addition to consolidation, however, the staff also saw an opportunity to augment the resiliency of the SAN architecture.

Today, local, direct-attached storage is still supported (there is no wholesale migration planned to get rid of DAS) when the application requirements can be met within the constraints of DAS functionality. There are three primary application requirements that dictate the need for a SAN-based infrastructure:

- Replication
- Multiple redundant paths
- Shared data storage (such as required by clustered file systems)

If any of the preceding features is required by an application, the application is built on SAN storage no matter the size. In other words, the architecture of the application is the most critical piece of the storage networking decision matrix.

Data Integrity and Resiliency

Many application environments at this firm are already resilient at the application level through the use of reliable multicast protocols, whereby the same data from an application is streamed to many different servers at one time. In the event of a server outage, the data is still transferred and the trade is still executed.

Financial institutions in the United States are governed explicitly by the Securities and Exchange Commission, but because this firm hosts data both in the United States as well as in Europe, it must adhere to rules from two different governing bodies. Data management practices at this firm, with regard to availability and disaster recovery, are regulated by both the SEC and United Kingdom's Financial Services Authority (FSA) and must meet stringent restrictions from both of those agencies.

This firm is currently in the process of validating proprietary replication software over Fibre Channel over IP (FCIP) on the Cisco IP Storage Services Modules to allow resiliency between London and Paris, and London and Chicago. After the FCIP implementation is complete, the firm will be fully redundant over the MDS switches with the capability to withstand up to two distinct component failures across the SAN fabric.

Each environment must be completely resilient so that no single component failure or disaster can take down all of the systems. Change control windows, as one might imagine, are extremely tight and maintenance updates and enhancements must be performed after hours and on weekends. Even with changes being performed after hours, resiliency is required to prevent failure stemming from human error.

To facilitate a redundant architecture, both the local SAN fabrics and those in the U.S. are mirrored, but completely separate. Changes performed in one environment are propagated to the other environments only after a period of time has passed. Because all port assignments are identical between each location to allow for failover in the event of a disaster, architectural decisions must be made inclusive of all environments—one-offs and ad-hoc changes are not permitted.

Storage Management

Similar to many other environments, day-to-day storage management at this firm is a group effort. Two individual subject matter experts are almost fully dedicated to caring for the core SAN infrastructure, while another six individuals manage provisioning requests. There is not, however, a dedicated storage team; instead, these individuals are part of a virtual storage administration team whose time is split between daily storage operations and systems ownership and management.

The goal of this team at this firm is to provide storage supply to meet storage demand as a service. This is accomplished through a storage utility model, whereby the virtual storage administrators assign storage from a pool monitored by the two subject matter experts who maintain the viability of the pool and the health of the core fabric.

To maximize resources, the firm chooses to shy away from implementing a strategy involving resources from a third vendor. If instituting a "second-vendor strategy" can be perceived as difficult because of related operational inefficiencies, a three-vendor strategy for networking and storage infrastructure is considered even more difficult. This firm likes the fact that Cisco was already integrated as the primary networking vendor, and they chose the Cisco storage networking products in part because of vendor integration (as well as for the support of multiple platforms in the same box).

Future Initiatives

The firm intends to complete an Internet Small Computer Systems Interface (iSCSI) pilot program in the second half of 2004, which will provide networked storage alternatives for host systems that might not necessarily justify the expense or performance of Fibre Channel connectivity.

NOTE   Recall the connectivity-cost conundrum discussed in previous chapters, whereby the cost of a single FC HBA can be more than the cost of some hosts.

Conclusion

The application infrastructure at this firm demonstrates the critical nature of IT at any financial institution. The use of storage networks and SAN extensions to build redundancy and increase availability—although specifically mandated for financial institutions by governing bodies—is widespread in any environment in which competition is rampant and the cost of downtime is immense. Businesses seeking maximum uptime for application infrastructure need to ensure that data is not only mirrored locally with redundant fabrics (as demonstrated in this case study), but also remotely replicated.

DECISION MAKER IMPLEMENTATION CHECKLIST

This presentation outlines eight principle steps for any storage networking implementation. I have used these processes for numerous multi-million dollar storage projects at Cisco. This list is not exhaustive; it provides only a generic skeleton around which one can build the formal processes and tactics required to execute a storage vision. You can find this presentation online at www.ciscopress.com/1587201186.

The goal of this presentation is to provide a framework in which to think about storage networking implementations and storage strategies in general, so that these basic concepts can be applied to any storage project in any IT environment.

The three storage strategies outlined in the presentation (migration, consolidation, and recovery) are the fundamental precepts of a successful storage vision. I find that many customers and end users consider these three strategies to have the most impact. In the past two years, Cisco has successfully implemented each of these strategies, which have helped pave the way for a cohesive and sustainable storage vision.

Every IT environment is different, and the Decision Maker Implementation Checklist—along with the TCO Calculator referenced in Appendix C, "TCO Calculator"—has been appropriately generalized to accommodate the many differences. Although the basic principles still apply to every organization, for optimal benefit, the checklist needs to be customized to best fit the methodologies of each individual environment.

THE BUSINESS CASE FOR STORAGE NETWORKS: STORAGE STRATEGIES FOR LOWERING TCO

The materials in this presentation (the definition of total cost of ownership [TCO], the overview of financial metrics, and how to apply them) are a microcosm of the entire book and reflect two years of work and study of the impact of storage strategies at various companies (including Cisco). The financial tools and strategies included are not specific to any one company, however, and can be used to measure the impact of storage initiatives in any environment.

You can find this presentation at www.ciscopress.com/1587201186.

TCO
CALCULATOR

I compiled my experiences with budgeting and capacity planning for enterprise storage environments into the TCO Calculator, which you can find at www.ciscopress.com/1587201186.

This tool uses simple calculations to create an estimate of an environment's storage TCO. Obviously this tool was designed with ease of use in mind; therefore, it tends to simplify many complex topics. The best results are achieved when the tool is customized for an environment based on data points specific to that environment. Generic examples are provided in Column B to help you determine what data should be entered in the cells in Column C.

Users need to first enable macros when opening the TCO Calculator, and when customizing or saving changes, users need to save the file under a different name to change the protected cells.

NOTE You can override lengthy calculations where indicated with the phrase *user entry*. Data entered here is added to the final total instead of the values calculated based on data entry (labeled auto-calculate).

The following sections explain the major fields in the TCO Calculator.

Capital Depreciation Schedule

In this field, you enter the number of months over which capital equipment is depreciated (typically 30 or 36). The TCO Calculator is designed to work only with the *straight-line* method of depreciation. If you use the *double-declining balance* method or another method of depreciation, you need to copy the tool to another location and customize it (after unlocking the appropriate cells).

Staffing Components

The calculations for Staffing Components are designed to measure the impact of costs associated with full-time, virtual, and contracting staff. Keep in mind that the cost of a fully burdened, full-time equivalent includes health insurance, 401(k), bonus, options, and so on, in addition to salary.

Storage Components

This portion of the tool is the most highly customized per environment. In loose terminology, the three types of storage change to architectures (direct-attached, SAN-attached, and network-attached) are treated as simple tiers.

NOTE   Note that SAN component costs are measured separately under Fibre Channel costs and that the acquisition costs for DAS and SAN can be the same.

Regardless of naming conventions, the assumption is that the enterprise has different types of storage deployed with different cost structures associated with each deployment.

If that is not the case, the user can enter only one type of generic storage and an accompanying acquisition cost. It is understood that acquisition costs decline over time and that any inventory of storage devices likely has different costs associated with it. This tool serves only as a snapshot of a period of up to one year.

Fibre Channel Components

The Fibre Channel Components section merely counts switch ports with a consideration for ports allocated as *interswitch links (ISLs)*. ISLs are treated as unutilized ports, although this is a gross over-simplification. This is simply a shorthand method of accounting for the costs associated with ISLs. For one year, the TCO is based on the depreciation schedule in cell C3.

Utilization Factor

Most users find that they must either leave the Utilization Factor values blank or make an educated guess about the allocation and utilization efficiencies.

Maintenance Components

Some users find that they know their yearly maintenance bills and do not need to go through the painful exercise of calculating the total bill based on monthly charges. These users should utilize the *user-entry* feature and enter the total maintenance costs instead of performing the default calculations for the Maintenance Components.

Host Component Costs

Obviously the Host Components Costs values are best guesses for users with large enterprise environments. At Cisco Systems, we have thousands of hosts, and at least half of them have Fibre Channel HBAs. This is, of course, only a best guess.

Facilities Expenses

Some users know their facilities costs, but most do not. In some cases, facilities staff can provide an estimate for budgetary purposes, but for most users, this number is a best guess based on the number of hosts and the number of datacenters. Real estate and utilities prices, which fluctuate wildly from location to location, have a significant change to impact on facilities expenses.

Cost of Downtime

This component will likely raise many questions. I based the calculation on an outage of one quarter of an hour. Feel free to customize this value as needed or leave it out entirely if it is unknown.

Backups

TCO calculations for backups are another hotly contested item. I have seen this one done a few different ways, but I chose to take the complexity out of this model. In this case, TCO is the number of tapes purchased in a year, the cost of each tape, the depreciation expense of the capital infrastructure (servers and libraries), and the annual cost of offsite tape storage and recall services. Measuring backup TCO can get unwieldy when the discussion leads to matters of tape retention, which can be from one year to seven years to forever. Keep in mind, the purpose of this tool is to take a snapshot of costs for one year only.

Network Infrastructure

The Network Infrastructure section attempts to account for the utilization of the network backbone as consumed by either Fibre Channel over IP (FCIP) or Internet SCSI (iSCSI) traffic. It is difficult to fine-tune this number; use your best guess or leave the value out if you wish.

INDEX

C

Title 21 Code of Federal Regulations,
  20
Toigo, John William
  The Holy Grail of Storage, 4
  utilization efficiencies, 26
tools, TCO Calculator fields, 226–230
total cost of ownership. *See TCO*
trade registration system (TRS), 215
TRS (trade registration system), 215

U

U.S. Bancorp Piper Jaffray Inc., 21
useful life, assets, 134
user entries, TCO calculator, 226
utilization, 56
  Cancer Therapy and Research
    Center, 164
  Cisco Systems, Inc., 197–199
  ISP (Internet service provider),
    178–179
  storage, 22, 26
    allocation efficiency, 26–29
    Cost of Poor Quality
      (COPQ), 23
    DAS (direct-attached
      storage), 24–25
    efficiency, 26–30
    yield, 23–24
Utilization Factor, TCO Calculator,
  228

V

value case analysis
  DAS-to-NAS migration, 79–81
  DAS-to-SAN migration, 72–76
  iSCSI implementation, 81–82
  storage consolidation, 76, 78
vendor selection, 103–104
  RFI (request for information),
    104–105
  RFP (request for proposal),
    105–106

  RFQ (request for quote), 105–106
Virtual Datacenter, 49
Virtual SAN (VSAN), 187
virtual storage teams, 108–109
virtualization, 135–136
  MonoSphere Storage Manager,
    137–138
VSAN (Virtual SAN), 187

W

WACC (weighted average
  cost-of-capital), 66
websites
  Cisco Press
    Decision Maker
      Implementation Checklist,
      222–224
    TCO Calculator, 226
  CTRC (Cancer Therapy and
    Research Center), 154
weighted average cost-of-capital
  (WACC), 66
World Wide Names (WWN), 170
WWN (World Wide Names), 170

X-Y-Z

XML (extensible markup language),
  94

yield, storage utilization, 22–24, 26
  allocation efficiency, 26–29
  Cost of Poor Quality (COPQ), 23
  DAS (direct-attached storage),
    24–25
  efficiency, 29–30